Miles Ahead

ED. WENDY COOLING

Cascades consultants:
John Mannion, former Head of English, London
Sheena Davies, Principal Teacher of English, Glasgow
Adrian Jackson, General English Advisor, West Sussex
Geoff Fox, Lecturer at the University of Exeter School of
    Education, and a National Curriculum Advisor
Emily Rought-Brooks, Head of English, London
Antonia Sharpe, English teacher, London

Other titles in the **Collins** *Cascades series that you might enjoy:*

War Stories: A *Cascades* collection of fiction and non-fiction

ED. CHRISTOPHER MARTIN

This collection from the author of the bestselling *War Poems* features accounts of war and its impact on human lives from before and after 1914, written by men and women. Suitable for GCSE and A-level work. ISBN 000 711 485 0

As it Happens: A *Cascades* collection of reportage

ED. ROSY BORDER

Fascinating and occasionally unbelievable first-hand accounts of great events, terrible situations and epic discoveries, selected by an experienced author and former journalist. ISBN 000 711 364 1

Wild World: A *Cascades* book of non-fiction

ED. ANNE GATTI

The natural world and the amazing field of scientific discovery have led to some powerful and influential writing over the years. This accessible and stimulating collection ranges from Darwin to Attenborough.

ISBN 000 711 166 5

For further information call 0870 0100442
fax 0141 306 3750
e-mail: Education@harpercollins.co.uk
website: www.CollinsEducation.com

ED. WENDY COOLING

Miles Ahead

((Collins

An imprint of HarperCollins*Publishers*

Published by HarperCollins*Publishers*,
77–85 Fulham Palace Rd, London W6 8JB

Selection © Wendy Cooling 2001

ISBN 000 711 259 9

First published in Great Britain by HarperCollins*Publishers* 2001

The right of Wendy Cooling to be identified as the editor of this work is
asserted.

With thanks to Christopher Martin and Antonia Sharpe.

British Library Cataloguing in Publication Data
A catalogue record for this book is available from the British Library.

Cover design by Ken Vail Graphic Design, Cambridge
Cover photograph by Stockmarket
Printed and bound in Hong Kong
Commissioned by Thomas Allain-Chapman
Edited by Gaynor Spry
Production by Katie Morris

Contents

Introduction

More and more people travel the world these days as the aeroplane has made it so much smaller than it once was. In the past travellers set off on journeys that lasted years to discover distant places. Now it is possible to take a day trip from London to Cairo – and to visit the pyramids after lunch!

Those who write about their journeys have tried to interpret the way of life in the lands they have passed through. They have tried to let the armchair traveller see the beauties of the natural environment, feel the wonder of great buildings and know the people they meet as they travel. They have tried to entertain us and to invite us to join with them in their adventure.

There are usually difficulties for the traveller to overcome and dangers to survive, yet as they return and tell their tales, they tell of astonishments and excitements, and gloss over the really tough times.

Today some of the journeys described in this book are not possible – Afghanistan is completely closed to foreign visitors and Burma becomes more and more isolated. Yet Rumania and Samarkand are easily accessible in these post-Soviet days, and China is more open to visitors. Travel writing over the years reflects an ever changing world and will surely continue to do so.

There is a strange power in new and different places that stimulates the imagination and makes it possible to put up with horrendous journeys and awful accommodation. There is, it seems, still much to be wondered at in the world and it is the travel writer who allows us to have just a small sense of that wonder.

This book offers small tastes of 21 books, books that are packed with ideas, insights and humour, and represent something of the wide range of travel writing available today. If any of these extracts touches your imagination, look for the book and read on. If, as you search for a particular title, your eye is caught by another, even more intriguing one, read on ... and on!

Beginnings

Why do so many people have a compulsive urge to travel or to read of the exploits of travellers from the comfort of their own armchair? The reasons could fill a book – some want to cross the hottest desert, be the first to a particularly inhospitable part of the world, to see ancient sites, to get into the record books, to escape for a while – or even to find material for a book! To open this small volume of journeys, or moments in journeys, let's look at just a small sample of the reasons for setting out.

Setting Off

In his book Around the World in 80 Days, *Jules Verne described a fictional journey undertaken by Phileas Fogg and his servant Passepartout, in 1872. Almost 116 years later, Michael Palin set off, not with a servant but with a television crew, to make a similar journey. By then, in 1988, it was possible to circumnavigate[1] the world by air in 36 hours, but planes were against the rules of this journey: the journey had to be made in 80 days using only transport that would have been available to Phileas Fogg. Michael Palin and his BBC team left London in style on 25 September 1988 as he describes in Day 1 of his diary – a diary that became a television series and a book.*

Michael Palin

from *Around the World in 80 Days* (1989)

> *Day 1   25 September*

I leave the Reform Club, Pall Mall, London one hundred and fifteen years three hundred and fifty-six days, ten and three-quarter hours after Phileas Fogg. It's a wet, stuffy morning, I've had three and a half hours sleep and the only thing I envy Phileas is that he's fictional.

Few buildings could be more fitted to a Great Departure. With its 60-foot-high main hall, marble columns, galleried arcades and the grand scale of a Renaissance palace the Reform Club is a place of consequence, grand and grave enough to add weight to any venture.

This morning it smells of old fish, and glasses and bottles from the night before stood around. I could see no one sampling the sort of breakfast Fogg had taken the day he left: '... a side dish, a boiled fish with Reading sauce of first quality, a scarlet slice of roast beef garnished with mushrooms, a rhubarb and gooseberry tart, and a bit of Chester

---

[1] **circumnavigate:** sail or fly completely around

cheese, the whole washed down with a few cups of that excellent tea, specially gathered for the stores of the Reform Club.'

I have tried to follow Fogg's example and travel light. 'Only a carpet bag,' he had instructed his servant Passepartout, 'in it two woollen shirts and three pairs of stockings … my mackintosh and travelling cloak, also stout shoes, although we shall walk but little or not at all.' I've managed to find a passable equivalent of a carpet bag and in it packed six shirts, six pairs of socks, six pairs of underpants, three T-shirts, a towel, a pair of swimming trunks, a short-sleeved sweater, three pairs of light trousers (long), two pairs ex-RAF trousers (short), a pair of sports shorts, a sponge bag, various pharmaceuticals, a change of shoes, a jacket and tie, a Sony Walkman, six cassettes, a small short-wave radio, a Panama hat and one or two heavy and serious books with which to improve my mind on long sea journeys. In a shoulder bag I carry my diary, a small dictaphone recorder for the on-the-spot notes, a camera, the BBC's *Get By In Arabic*, a Kingsley Amis novel, some extra-strong mints, a packet of 'Family Wipes', an address book and an inflatable globe to enable me to check on our progress. Phileas Fogg would doubtless have regarded all this as clutter, but it's still less than I would take on a two-week holiday.

These bags I heave up onto my shoulders as the clock shows ten o'clock. I carry them down the stairs, out of the tall doorway and into Pall Mall. I've eighty days to get back in again.

Fogg went from the Reform Club to Charing Cross station, I leave from Victoria.

Here I find Passepartout, who will travel everywhere with me. Unlike Fogg's Passepartout, mine is five people, has fifty pieces of baggage and works for the BBC. Roger Mills is the director of this first leg of the journey and is already bemoaning the fact that we've just missed some foul weather in the English Channel. 'If only this had been yesterday.' He draws on his pipe despondently. Ann Holland is his Production Assistant. She will keep full details of all the shots we take, and keep in touch with our base camp in London. Nigel Meakin and Julian Charrington are the camera team and Ron Brown is recording sound. The film equipment is in containers of many shapes and sizes and mostly very heavy. As I help them down the platform with a muscle-tearing case of film stock I think of Phileas – 'one of those mathematically exact people ... never hurried ... calm, phlegmatic, with a clear eye' – and how desperately unlike him I am.

However, I am leaving London in a manner of which he would doubtless have approved had it been available in 1872, aboard the Venice-Simplon Orient Express. Last farewells and a check on the exact time of departure by two friends acting as judges. Fogg's friends were bankers. Mine, Messrs Jones and Gilliam, are Pythons. Terry Jones eyes Passepartout, already about his business with the camera. 'You're going to have to look happy for eighty days.' 'No,' I reassure him. 'There'll be no cheating.' Then the whistle sounds, the last door slams and we're off.

I am installed in a sumptuous refurbished Pullman coach called 'Zena'. Behind me are 'Ibis', 'Lucille', 'Cygnus' and 'Ione'. Antimacassars,[2] marble washbasins, upholstered armchairs and inlaid walnut panelling come as a bit of a shock to one used to the Gatwick Express, but I try hard to forget about guilt and silly things like that and sit back and sniff the fresh orchids and sip a little champagne. The leader of a crack force of waiters approaches, issuing brisk directives.

'We *do* advise you to be seated. We're coming through the train with hot soup.'

We are dealt a three-course meal and coffee in 55 minutes flat. It's delicious, but such is the precision with which it has to be served that you feel that any lingering over the menu might result in the afore-mentioned hot soup being lightly but firmly applied upon some tender area.

A huge scar slices into the landscape on the eastern side of the train. It's the site for the Channel Tunnel terminal, 16 acres of devastation. Jules

---

[2] **antimacassars**: cloths covering the backs and arms of chairs

Verne would surely have approved, being a man fascinated by transport technology. He'd probably have sent his hero to have a look at it. Or rather, he'd have sent Passepartout to do it for him, as Fogg hated sightseeing.

We're in Folkestone now, the last few hundred yards of England, and rumbling down a steep gradient past back gardens close up to the railway line; a world of sheds and extensions, corrugated iron and chicken wire, unselfconscious, domestic and reassuring. The sun breaks momentarily through the leaden cloud causing the mountain of cut-glass on my table to sparkle, but the word is that the Channel is 'rough' to 'very rough', and I'm glad I passed on the ginger profiteroles.

No longer do the ferries carry trains and at Folkestone Harbour I part company with 'Zena' and take up with the *Horsa*, a 6000-ton vessel which has been plying the 22-mile crossing to France for 16 years.

'It's that Monty Python bloke!' shouts one of the crew as I mount the first of many gangplanks of the world. He turns confidingly to me: 'If you want a farce, you've got one here.' The passageways of the *Horsa* smell of day-old school food, but we Oriental Expressers are ushered to our private lounge.

It's a dispiriting place, decorated in International Cowboy Saloon Style. The walls are ringed with reverentially lit alcoves which look as if they might contain international art treasures or religious icons, but which, on closer inspection, are found to be full of duty-free goods.

Seeking refuge from the world of 'Antaeus, Pour Homme' and 'Superkings', I walk out on deck. It's mid-afternoon and the white cliffs of home are now little more than a blur. A huge black cloud seems to be sealing England off behind us. A sharp, squally wind that would test the stoutest toupee rips across from the West. With friends and familiar surroundings disappearing over the horizon, I catch my breath for a moment at the scale of what is just beginning.

The Channel crossing is bumpy, but to the director's chagrin nothing more. A Force 5. 'I've had her out in a Force 12,' says the captain, eyes skinned for stray fishing boats, tankers, ferries, yachts, channel-swimmer's support vessels and every floating thing that makes this one of the busiest waterways in the world.

4.30: On the bridge. From a mile out at sea Boulogne, France, looks to consist of one huge steelworks, but as we get nearer a hard skyline of soot-flecked concrete apartment blocks looms.

Down below, the Orient Express passengers are impatient to party. They so want to have a good time, and the expensive hours are ticking away and the luxury they were promised is not to be found on the *Horsa* or in the passageways of Boulogne's dockside. But spirits rise once they reach the platform of Boulogne station at which stand a dozen coaches sporting the navy-blue livery and solid brass letters of the Compagnie Internationale des Wagons-Lits et des Grands Express Européens. I am billeted in sleeping car 3544, built in 1929, decorated in 'Sapelli Pearl' inlay by René Prou and having been, in the course of a long and distinguished career, a brothel for German officers and part of the Dutch royal train. My cabin is small but perfectly formed, sheathed in veneered mahogany inlaid with Art-Deco panels. From this luxury cocoon I watch grey, seagull-ridden Boulogne slipping away and when its drab suburbs have gone, I turn once more to make-believe, and begin unpacking my dinner jacket.

I dine next to a couple from Southend who are celebrating their twenty-fifth wedding anniversary with an Orient Express trip to Paris. Nice people but, looking round, I'm rather disappointed at the lack of princesses, murderers and deposed heads of Europe. Most of the 188 passengers are either going to a pipeline conference in Venice or are Mid-Westerners on a tour. Instead of falling into risqué conversation with a Mata Hari[3] of the 1980s, I end up in the piano bar with the pipeliners. They seem very interested to hear that, in seventy days from now, I hope

---

[3] **Mata Hari:** Dutch dancer who was executed as a German spy in the First World War

to cross the Atlantic from Halifax, Nova Scotia. 'We've got a big pipe there, we could flush you through.'

My cabin has been prepared for the night by Jeff, a down-to-earth, well-informed Englishman who has responsibility for Coach 3544. The bed is soft but short. 'Yes, we do have a bit of trouble with our Americans,' he concedes. 'There's one tonight who's 6 foot 8.' He looks apprehensively down the corridor, listening no doubt for the giant's tread. Feeling for the first time in my life rather smug about being 5 foot 10 and a half, I turn in. The train is heading for the Belfort Gap, my head is buzzing with an evening's champagne, and so far circumnavigation is a doddle.

Ⓐ *See pages 112–113 for related activities.*

A Forbidden Land

Katie Hickman spent her childhood on the move, living in Spain, the Far East, Southern Ireland, Chile and Equador. Travel was in her blood and as soon as she graduated from university she was on the move again.

Her journey to the isolated land of Bhutan started with a book but really happened simply because Bhutan was a forbidden land. I too travelled to Bhutan – because of a radio programme that described the life of a postman there, a postman who climbed for a whole day to deliver letters to a particular monastery! His life and what he said about Bhutan fascinated me and stuck in my mind and I, like Katie Hickman, simply had to go. Katie Hickman makes her living as a travel writer and wrote about her journey around Bhutan in Dreams of the Peaceful Dragon.

Katie Hickman

from *Dreams of the Peaceful Dragon* (1987)

In the Beginning

I have never been much good at beginnings. For a start, with this journey in particular, I am in several minds as to where the beginning began. I could, of course, take the easy way out and start chronologically at the exact moment when I arrived in Bhutan, but, you see, that is not it at all.

A friend of mine suggested that if I could not think of a suitably dramatic beginning then the best thing I could do would be to invent one. Travel books, she said, were perfectly legitimate outlets for invention, for fantasy, and great fertile leaps of the imagination; in any case, the truth was bound to be far too dull.

So why should I have wanted to go to Bhutan in the first place? It was a chance encounter of a kind, not with a person but with a book, which gave me a clue to the fascination Bhutan exerts. It was a short biography, only a few pages long, of a man called Thomas Manning.

Manning was an eccentric traveller who at the beginning of the nineteenth century was one of the first Europeans ever to enter the unknown kingdom of Bhutan *en route* for China and Tibet. While he was at Cambridge Manning had become so obsessed with the idea of the East, that he resolved to enter it 'at all hazards, and to prosecute his researches until death stopped him, or until he should return with success'. Charles Lamb, who was a close friend of Manning's, was horrified by this notion of visiting 'Independent Tartary', and did his best to dissuade him from going. His half-jesting argument was that the reading of Chaucer had misled his friend with its foolish stories of Cambuscan and the ring and the horse of brass.

'Believe me,' he wrote, 'there are no such things. 'Tis all the poet's invention. A horse of brass never flew, and a king's daughter never talked with birds. These are all tales. Pray try and cure yourself. Take hellebore.[1] Pray to avoid the fiend. Read no more books of voyages, they are nothing but lies.'

When I read this I realised that Charles Lamb had missed the point. We do not only travel to find the truth, but also to rediscover the mysteries that are in life. Ours is a world in which few stones remained unturned. Even the Man in the Moon has been walked on, and his enigmatic smile has been analysed, explained.

The world has few secrets left, but Bhutan is one of them. This is why I went there.

Bhutan is a country that every traveller dreams of: a tiny mountaintop kingdom, the great buttresses of the Himalayas surrounding it like a fortress. Only 18,000 square miles, the country is bordered to the south and east by the Indian states of Bengal, Assam and Arunachal Pradesh, and to the west by the once independent principality of Sikkim, now gobbled up by and forming part of India. It is to the North, however, that

---

[1] **hellebore:** a plant used in the treatment of heart disease

Bhutan looks most closely, to the vast frozen wastelands of its cultural and spiritual homeland: to Tibet.

Throughout the long-petrified centuries of its existence, Bhutan has remained so isolated that until relatively recently the western world did not even have a name for it. The word 'Bhutan' is an anglicisation of the old Sanskrit term 'Bhotana', which referred loosely to the whole, but only dimly perceived, area of Tibet and its barbarian fringes. In turn, the ancient scribes of Tibet alluded, perhaps enviously, to its lush, fertile valleys by a number of different names, calling it 'The Paradise of the South', 'The Land of Hidden Treasures' and 'The Southern Valleys of the Medicinal Herbs'. The Bhutanese themselves call their country Druk Yul. It means The Land of the Thunder Dragon.

Until the early 1970s Bhutan was not only almost completely unknown by the outside world, but also unknowable. Its eyrie-like location has made it one of the most inaccessible countries in the world, and it has been possessively guarded against intruders and travellers alike by the Bhutanese themselves. The country perches between India and China, and its people have always been suspicious of even the most innocent intrusions by outsiders. With both Sikkim and Tibet now irretrievably swallowed up into the giant maws of these neighbours, Bhutan can hardly be blamed. Against all the odds it has succeeded in remaining an independent state, and, perhaps more remarkably, in retaining its ancient culture untainted, and in all its original potency. Bhutan's methods of ensuring this have been Draconian.[2] For three hundred years, from its unification in the seventeenth century until the early 1970s, the country followed a policy of self-imposed isolation from the outside world. Few Bhutanese ever left their country; even fewer outsiders were ever allowed in. It was a forbidden land.

---

[2] **Draconian:** harsh

Ⓐ *See pages 112–113 for related activities.*

All For a Bet

In 1988 Tony Hawks published a book entitled Round Ireland with a
Fridge. *It tells of a very different journey, one undertaken because of a
bet made on an over-the-top night out: 'I hereby bet Tony Hawks the
sum of One Hundred Pounds that he cannot hitch-hike round the
circumference of Ireland, with a fridge, within one calendar month.'
Not as long a journey as Michael Palin's, but one with a seriously
awkward encumbrance instead of a team of supporters. Tony Hawks's
journey is a romp, full of humour, fun and friendly encounters but one
that is rarely easy.*

Tony Hawks
from *Round Ireland with a Fridge* (1998)

Shane must be a very good friend of Seamus. I can just imagine his face
when he got the call.

'Oh hi Shane, it's Seamus here – could you do a favour for me?'
'Sure.'

He had already made mistake number one by not finding out the
nature of the favour first.

'There's this friend of mine Tony and he's going to hitch-hike round
Ireland with a fridge.'

'Hmmmmm.'

'Could you buy a small fridge and a trolley for it and pick him up at
Dublin airport? He'll give you the money when he gets there.'

'Er–'

'Good, grand ... I'll ring you Friday with the flight details.'

And there he was at the airport, the man who had been entrusted with
the responsibility of purchasing someone's travelling companion for the

next month, a role more commonly associated with Bangkok than Dublin. Although we'd never met, we knew each other instantly. He must have been able to recognise the wild apprehension in my eyes and I could see the dismay in his. He greeted me cordially enough and we made our way to the car. That was where the fridge was, he told me, accurately assessing that its whereabouts were my main concern.

I was rather nervous about meeting it. He'd been given detailed instructions and he seemed bright enough, but what if he'd bought the wrong kind of fridge? I suddenly felt it had been a mistake to have abdicated responsibility for this, the most important of all my pieces of baggage. After all I knew so much about fridges having been given the lowdown by an expert like Darren. But it had to be like this because today was a Sunday and not a good day for fridge shopping, and I wanted to make a start first thing in the morning. It was almost like starting a new job – in on Monday morning, bright and early, looking your best and keen to impress.

We climbed the stairs in the surprisingly odourless multi-storey car park. I found Shane to be a reticent man but assumed he was more so today because his thoughts were occupied trying to work out the size of the favour he would demand from Seamus in return for having done this one. It was certain to be a biggy, along the lines of 'There's this man I want you to kill ...' Then I saw the fridge for the first time. Shane had done well. Exactly what I had been looking for, a white cube about two feet square. I patted it affectionately and Shane looked away allowing us a moment of intimacy. Then he produced the trolley and in reverent silence we strapped the fridge to it, respectful witnesses at the birth of a truly symbiotic relationship.

I wheeled the fridge around the car park a bit like a sportsman warming up, and it felt good. Me, the fridge and the trolley were going to get along just fine. We would have been the dream team if it hadn't been for the rucksack. Initiation ceremony out of the way we headed off. Shane had exceeded his initial brief by organising bed and breakfast accommodation in an area south of the River Liffey called Donnybrook. He started to relax and we chatted more freely. He revealed himself to be quite amused by my prospective expedition and suggested that I get in touch with a radio show on RTE FM 2 called *The Gerry Ryan Show*. He said that they liked to get behind wacky ventures and mine fitted the bill perfectly. I hadn't thought of doing anything like that but as we progressed slowly through the gridlocked centre of Dublin the idea grew on me.

We reached Donnybrook and I paid Shane the £130 I owed him for the fridge.

'By the way, how much is the bet for?' he asked.

'A hundred pounds,' I replied.

He was confused for a moment, then he rather hurriedly wished me good luck and drove off with a look on his face that suggested that he was relieved that I wasn't in his car anymore.

I was greeted at the B&B by Rory, a young man who looked as if he'd just graduated and was some way from being the middle-aged maternal lady called Rosie who I imagined ran all these kinds of establishments. He had very thick lenses in his glasses and I found the resulting enlargement of his eyes a little disconcerting. He declared that he had no problems on the vacancy front given that he had no other guests staying. Initially he didn't comment as I wheeled the fridge into his hall, but he surveyed it in such a way as to suggest that he wasn't confident that his thick lenses were thick enough. A few seconds passed and he capitulated.

'Is that a fridge?' he said.

This was an enquiry I was to hear a good deal more in the weeks to come.

'Yes,' I replied accurately.

He didn't pursue this line of questioning and I offered nothing further although I could tell that he was curious. I had made a decision before leaving that I would try not to volunteer information about this fridge unless it was asked of me and then I would tell the truth. I was interested to see how many people wouldn't ask, either through politeness or a general lack of interest. Rory fell into the former category.

Shortly after I'd settled into my room and was embarking on some gentle unpacking there was a knock on the door. It was Rory asking me if I would do him a favour. I carelessly said 'no problem' in a manner of which Shane would have been proud. Rory said that he was popping out for a while and would I mind answering the phone if it went, and once again I obliged with another 'no problem'. Forty minutes and three bookings later, I decided that the best course of action was to go out myself.

I was feeling pretty jaded, with recent sleepless nights and the trauma of the flight taking their toll, but I had two things I wanted to do before I turned in for the night. Firstly, since Shane had pointed out that the RTE studios were fortuitously only five minutes walk away, I saw no harm in dropping a note into *The Gerry Ryan Show* giving them details of the journey I was about to embark on and leaving the phone number of Rory's B&B if they wanted to speak to me in the morning.

I dropped my explanatory letter into RTE, ate a disappointing take-away, returned to Rory's, took a shower and went to bed. Fortunately I was so tired that it didn't take me long to fall asleep. If it had, I might have started to become anxious about what the next day held in store.

The next morning I was woken by Rory knocking on my door. I *thought*, 'Oh God, I suppose you're going out again and you want me to man the telephones and make my own breakfast?' but *said*, 'Yes?'

Not such a good line but it came a close second.

'Phonecall for you,' said an excited Rory, 'it's *The Gerry Ryan Show*.'

'Oh. Right.'

Having been awake only a matter of seconds I wasn't exactly on top of what all this meant. I opened the door and Rory handed me one of those cordless phones which nearly always get a bad reception however much the manufacturers promise otherwise. I put it to my ear.

'Hello?'

'Hello Tony, it's Siobhan here from *The Gerry Ryan Show*, I'll put you on hold and you'll be though to Gerry in a minute.'

Gerry? I don't know a Gerry. And why can't he talk to me now? Before I could say anything I found myself listening to Chris Rea and the whole thing dawned on me. Oh no, I was going to be on air after this record! What about my hair? I cleared my throat several times in an effort to make it sound less like I'd just woken up. I tried to ignore Chris Rea's lyrics; after all the thought of being on 'the road to hell' was disturbing enough first thing in the morning, but when you were about to embark on a venture like mine it was almost as if the bastard was taking the piss.

Gerry Ryan's voice cut through the fading record.

'Now, I've got Tony Hawks on the line. Good morning Tony – now you're about to make an interesting journey – would you care to tell us about it?'

I can think of easier things to do one minute after you've woken up.

Actually I didn't do a bad job of explaining what I was up to and why, even managing to be faintly amusing from time to time.

'I've no idea if I'll stay this jolly,' I said to Gerry at one stage, 'it's only because I haven't started yet that I sound this happy.'

'Well, I think maybe if the weather is good for you, you'll probably get a very good response, and indeed knowing the way the national psyche of the people in this country works, you'll probably be made extremely welcome – and it will be a great thing for the peace process.'

'Well, I hope to be passing through Northern Ireland later today, so if I can do anything to smooth things over up there I'd be more than happy – maybe we should all get around the fridge. People have tried getting round tables and it doesn't really work out, the whole body language thing behind a table is all wrong – so let's all get round the fridge.'

'I think you may have hit on something there, Tony – that could be our motto for the peace process – "Let's get round the fridge".'

We must have chatted for six or seven minutes, which surprised me because I was so used to English radio where they want a few quick soundbytes from you before they whack on another record. We even took a call from a pub landlord offering to throw a 'fridge party' when I got to Cork. I thanked him and promised to take him up on the offer, but wondered if he had any idea as to what a fridge party might involve. It didn't seem to matter.

In Gerry Ryan I could tell I was dealing with a very accomplished broadcaster who had mastered the art of calmly coping with four things happening at once whilst talking at the same time. He also seemed to be genuinely intrigued by the absurdity of my undertaking and wound up the interview by saying, 'This is exactly the kind of thing that we like to keep an eye on – we will put the full weight of RTE behind you, will you call us tomorrow?'

'Absolutely, Gerry, I'd be delighted.'

'Good morning.'

'Good morning.'

I sounded very happy and indeed I was. But only because I hadn't woken up properly, both in the physical and metaphorical sense, to the reality of what lay ahead of me. Furthermore I hadn't looked out of the window so I was blissfully unaware that it was sheeting down with rain.

Through the phone's earpiece I heard Gerry's summing up, 'Good luck to Tony ... well, you have to say it's a completely purposeless idea, but a damn fine one.'

I hoped that the rest of Ireland would feel the same.

A *See pages 112–113 for related activities.*

Sights and Sounds

Most travellers, especially those who write down their experiences, come back with a head full of images, images that can be difficult to share because the smells and sounds that were part of the scene are hard to express in words. Many like to travel because distant, very difficult places can touch all the senses and leave no room for everyday thoughts; many talk of India as a land that batters all the senses at once leaving behind a feeling of wonder – and exhaustion!

Paradise in the Panjshir Valley

Eric Newby has travelled widely, especially in Europe and Asia, and has written fascinating accounts of his journeys. In this extract he remembers a moment in Afghanistan when he felt himself to be in paradise.

Eric Newby

from *A Short Walk in the Hindu Kush* (1958)

Descending swiftly from our vehicle, we drank tea on the balcony of a *chaie khana*[1] which hung on its stilts over the little Shatul river, which came purling down into the town between narrow banks. The tea place was beside the bridge at the junction of three roads and from its shelter we could watch the life of the little town.

Sitting with their backs to us on the wall of the bridge five ancient men, old Tajiks, with dyed beards, sat motionless. On the opposite side of the river, twenty feet away from us in another tea-house a band of Pathans, their eyes dyed with an extract from the plant called madder, carried on an animated conversation, passing a water pipe from hand to hand until, feeling themselves watched, they glared at us suspiciously.

The air was full of cries, outlandish smells of smoke and animals, dust and excitement. A bus gaily painted like a fantastic dragonfly and laden to suffocation point with passengers, failed to make the sharp turn and became jammed at the entrance to the bridge just at the moment when a flock of sheep, several hundreds strong, coming from the mountains also debouched on it.[2] The noise was deafening as the sheep, mad with fear, tried to nuzzle the old men over the pediment[3] of the bridge and into the water below, but they sat stolidly on.

---

[1] **chaie khana:** tea-house
[2] **debouched on it:** flowed onto it
[3] **pediment:** pointed gable end

There was an interval of calm while five women, saucy ghosts in all-enveloping *chador*,[4] with crocheted holes for faces, rode over the bridge on horseback, each with an anxious-looking husband trotting behind on foot.

They were succeeded by two urchins who fought strenuously in the dust, ripping great chunks out of one another's already ragged clothing. Then, quite suddenly, the road was deserted and a young man appeared strutting slowly and stiffly with both arms held straight down in front of him. He was almost goose-stepping and he was completely naked. For some minutes he stood in the middle of the bridge with fingers extended, holding up the traffic.

No one, including the five old men, took the slightest notice of him. He went slowly up the road at the head of a small procession of men, animals and vehicles that had been piling up, waiting for him to make up his mind where he wanted to go, and disappeared. Lunatic, *Darwish* from some strange sect, or simply someone from the city come to take the waters of the Shatul (well known for their medicinal qualities) who had lost his bath towel, we shall never know. Even the omniscient Ghulam Naabi, who went off to interrogate the inhabitants, returned no wiser.

We came to the mouth of the Panjshir gorge from which the river raced, shooting down with little scuds of foam, brilliant in the sun. It was an exciting moment. Ahead of us the mountains rose straight up like a wall. Those on the left, towards the west, formed part of the Hindu Kush range; those to the right, separated by fifty yards of the rushing water that had cut this gorge, were the final spurs of the great massif,[5] itself a spur of the Hindu Kush that projects southwards from the Anjuman Pass at the head of the Panjshir Valley, forming the western marches of Nuristan in which was Mir Samir, our mountain.

---

[4] **chador:** large shawls or veils
[5] **massif:** series of connected rocks

I took one last look at the smiling plain behind us with its rich market gardens and the mountains to the west where the sun was beginning to sink, then we were in the cold shadow of the gorge with the river thundering about us, cold and green and white, sucking and tugging at the great boulders that lay in the stream, the noise of it reverberating from the walls thirty yards from side to side like the entrance to a tomb. After about a mile the gorge suddenly opened out into a valley where the mountains were no longer sheer but ran back in steep banks of scree.

As we drove on we had momentary glimpses of jagged peaks. They were as dry as old bones; there was no snow or ice to be seen – that would be farther back, higher still in the Hindu Kush.

The road turned a corner and now, on the far bank of the river, infinitely secret-looking villages with watch towers built of dried mud, loop-holed and with heavily barred windows, clung to the mountain-side. We turned another corner and suddenly were in paradise.

It was evening but the last of the sun drenched everything in golden light. In a field of Indian corn women were slyly using their veils. They no longer wore the wraithlike *chador* that we had seen in Gulbahar and Kabul. In the small terraced fields, which fitted into one another like a jig-saw or, when they were at different levels, like some complicated toy, the wheat was being harvested by men using sickles. From the fields donkeys moved off uphill in single file to the tomb-like villages, so loaded that they looked like heaps of wheat moved by clockwork.

But it was the river that dominated the scene. In it boys were swimming held up by inflated skins and were swept downstream in frightening fashion until the current swirled them into deep pools near the bank before any harm could come to them; while in the shallows where the water danced on pebbles smaller children splashed and pottered. On its banks, too, life was being lived happily: a party of ladies in reds and brilliant blues walked along the opposite bank, talking gaily to one another; poplars shimmered; willows bowed in the breeze; water flowed slowly in the irrigation ditches through a hundred gardens, among apricot trees with the fruit still heavy on them, submerging the butts of the mulberries, whose owners squatted in their properties and viewed the scene with satisfaction. Old white-bearded men sat proudly on stone walls with their grandchildren, grave-looking little boys with embroidered pill-box hats and little girls of extraordinary beauty. This evening was like some golden age of human happiness, attained sometimes by children, more rarely by grown-ups, and it communicated its magic in some degree to all of us.

The road wriggled on and on. It was like driving along the back of a boa-constrictor that had just enjoyed a good meal, and equally bumpy. At Ruka, the principal town of the lower Panjshir, the main street through the bazaar was covered in with the boughs of trees to form a dark tunnel in which the shopkeepers had already lit acetylene flares. It was not yet the time for custom and the owners of the stall-like shops sat cross-legged and motionless, waiting; proprietors of *chaie khanas* with their big brass samovars[6] boiling up behind them and shelves of massed teapots; butchers in their shops where legs of mutton, still black with the day's flies, hung from cruel-looking hooks; sellers of shoes with curly toes, rock salt in blocks, strange clothing – all ready for business. In the middle of the bazaar, chocked up on tree-trunks, without wheels stood an enormous American automobile of the thirties, the reputed property of a German who had gone prospecting over the Anjuman Pass and who had not returned.

---

[6] **samovars:** urns for making tea

Ⓐ *See pages 114–116 for related activities.*

Port of Spain, Trinidad

V.S. Naipaul (b.1931) is a great traveller and novelist, essayist and travel writer. He was born in Trinidad and later settled in England – but perhaps 'settled' is the wrong word for someone so often on the move. He has the extraordinary ability to take readers right into a place and to bring it absolutely to life in wonderful word pictures. Here he describes the Trinidad he returns to after a long absence and how he is taken aback by the sounds that fill his head.

V.S. Naipaul

from *The Middle Passage* (1962)

Port of Spain is the noisiest city in the world. Yet it is forbidden to talk. 'Let the talkies do the talking,' the signs used to say in the old London Theatre of my childhood. And now the radios and the rediffusion sets[1] do the talking, the singing, the jingling; steel bands do the booming and the banging; and the bands, live or tape-recorded, and the gramophones and record-players. In restaurants the bands are there to free people of the need to talk. Stunned, temples throbbing, you champ and chew, concentrating on the working of your jaw muscles. In a private home as soon as anyone starts to talk the radio is turned on. It must be loud, loud. If there are more than three, dancing will begin. Sweat-sweat-dance-dance-sweat. Loud, loud, louder. If the radio isn't powerful enough, a passing steel band will be invited in. Jump-jump-sweat-sweat-jump. In every house a radio or rediffusion set is on. In the street people conduct conversations at a range of twenty yards or more; and even when they are close to you their voices have a vibrating tuning-fork edge. You will realise this only after you have left Trinidad: the voices in British

---

[1] ***rediffusion sets:*** televisions

Guiana will sound unnaturally low, and for the first day or so whenever anyone talks to you you will lean forward conspiratorially, for what is being whispered is, you feel, very secret. In the meantime dance, dance, shout above the shuffle. If you are silent the noise will rise to a roar about you. You cannot shout loud enough. Your words seem to be issuing from behind you. You have been here only an hour, but you feel as exhausted as though you had spent a day in some Italian scooter-hell. Your head is bursting. It is only eleven; the party is just warming up. You are being rude, but you must go.

You drive up the new Lady Young Road, and the diminishing noise makes it seem cooler. You get to the top and look out at the city glittering below you, amber and exploding blue on black, the ships in the harbour in the background, the orange flames issuing from the oil derricks[2] far out in the Gulf of Paria. For a moment it is silent. Then, above the crickets, whose stridulation[3] you hadn't noticed, you begin to hear the city: the dogs, the steel bands. You wait until the radio stations have closed down for the night – but rediffusion sets, for which there is a flat rental, are never turned off: they remain open, to await the funnelling of the morning noise – and then you wind down into the city again, drowning in the din. All through the night the dogs will go on, in a thousand inextricably snarled barking relays, rising and falling, from street to street and back again, from one end of the city to another. And you will wonder how you stood it for eighteen years, and whether it was always like this.

---

[2] **oil derricks:** oil platforms
[3] **stridulation:** noise produced by rubbing one part of the body against another

🅐 *See pages 114–116 for related activities.*

Nyika Plateau

The late Sir Laurens van der Post (1906–1996) was a farmer, writer and traveller. His home was in South Africa but he travelled widely throughout Africa, and his books and articles reflect a real love and knowledge of that continent. This extract lets us see something of the wildlife of Africa.

Sir Laurens van der Post

from *A Book of Travellers' Tales* (1952)

There was no wind any more. There was no cloud or mist in the sky. I have never known such stillness. The only sound was the sound of one's blood murmuring like a far sea in one's ears: and that serene land and its beauty, and the level golden sunlight seemed to have established such a close, delicate, tender communion with us that the murmur in my ears seemed also like a sound from without; it was like a breathing of the grasses, a rustle of the last shower of daylight, or the swish of the silk of evening across the purple slopes.

Suddenly Karramba touched my arm. We could hardly believe our eyes. A very big male leopard, bronze, his back charged with sunset gold, was walking along the slope above the pool on the far side about fifty yards away. He was walking as if he did not have a fear or care in the world, like an old gentleman with his hands behind his back, taking the evening air in his own private garden. When he was about twelve yards from the pool, he started walking around in circles examining the ground with great attention. Then he settled slowly into the grass, like a destroyer sinking into the sea, bow first, and suddenly disappeared from our view. It was rather uncanny. One minute he was magnificently there on the bare slope and the next he was gone from our view …

We waited attentively. About five minutes passed: not a sound anywhere, except this remote music of all our being. I was lying with my ear close to the ground when I heard a new sound that made my heart beat faster: it was the drumming of hooves far away. It was a lovely, urgent, wild barbaric sound. It was getting louder and coming straight for us. I caught a glimpse of Michael's face, shining with excitement. The drumming of the hooves came towards us from somewhere behind the far slope, like a great Pacific comber,[1] like a charge of Napoleon's cavalry at Waterloo, and then out of the midst of this drumming, this surf of sound, there was thrown up like a call on a silver trumpet, or the voice of an emperor born to command, a loud, clear neigh. It was one of the most beautiful sounds I have ever heard, and it established itself in all my senses like the far silver fountain that I had once seen a great blue whale throw up on a South Atlantic horizon after a storm. Now, as the sun tinted the horizon, the wave of sound rose towering into the air and then crashed down on to the summit of the slope opposite us. A troop of about forty zebra, running as if they had never known walking, the rhythm of their speed moving in waves across their shining flanks, charged over the crest and made for the pool where the leopard lay.

I wondered how it was going to end. I could not believe a leopard would attack such a lusty group of zebra, although I had never seen a leopard behave quite as this one did, so frankly, so openly. At that very moment, the leader of the troop with his mane streaming from him like the strands of the Mistral[2] itself, stopped dead. At one minute he must have been going at thirty-five miles an hour, at the next he stopped without a slither in his tracks, two fountains of steam shooting out of his dilated nostrils.

The rest of the group stopped with him. Had they seen the leopard or seen us? For about five minutes we saw a group of zebra, not fifty yards away, in earnest consultation. I saw Michael raise his gun and then put it

[1] **comber:** long curling wave
[2] **Mistral:** wind that blows trough the Rhône valley and southern France

down again. He had, I knew, to kill one zebra because it was his duty to examine them for parasites. I saw him take aim several times but always he put his gun down again.

Meanwhile the consultation went on, soundlessly and ceaselessly. Some invisible, some electric exchange of meaning was going on between those vivid creatures on the darkening slope. They looked so heraldic, like unicorns who had just had their horns pared. They had beautifully marked golden skins, with black blazonings. For five minutes they stood, their steaming heads close together, and then somewhere in the magnetic depths of themselves, their meaning fused and became one. They whirled swiftly round and charged back over the crest straight into the dying day and we did not see them again.

'I am sorry,' Michael said to me, breathing hard: 'I am sorry but I just could not shoot: they were beautiful.'

'I am glad you didn't,' I answered.

Ⓐ *See pages 114–116 for related activities.*

In Samarkand

Great Railway Journeys of the World *has been made into a television series as well as a book. There is something wonderful about seeing the world through train windows and stopping at sleepy, unheard-of places as well as at great towns.*

The following extract is by the ballerina, Natalia Makarova, who journeyed from St Petersburg to Tashkent, from the icy Gulf of Finland to the heat of Central Asia. Here she arrives in one of the most beautiful places in the world, Samarkand, and recounts the legend of the Bibi mosque – a story also told to me by an Imam as I sat gazing at the scene around me. His version was not quite the same as Natalia's, it had a kinder ending. In the story I heard, Tamerlane forgave his wife but ordered her to wear a veil so that no other man would be tempted by her beauty – and, even happier, the architect, being the cleverest in the world, escaped punishment by making himself a pair of wings and flying off to the safety of a distant land.

Natalia Makarova
from *Great Railway Journeys of the World* (1994)

We awake in Samarkand. Venturing into the city is like stepping into a vividly-coloured dream, with exotic fruits, flowing silks and cerulean blue domes lending their hues to the swirling confusion of colour. Samarkand today is a unique blend of legend and history. In olden times the capital of several powerful states, it has been called the 'Eden of the Orient' and the 'Glittering summit of the world'; Tamerlane called it the 'eye and star of the earth'.

Ruy de Clavijo, a Spanish traveller who visited Tamerlane's court, wrote this in his journal: 'As I was approaching Samarkand, I searched to find a metaphor to describe its beauty. And I said "Samarkand is like the colour of the sky, with its palaces shining like stars, and its streams flowing like the Milky Way!" and everybody liked what I said.'

The architectural monuments are breathtaking in their bold design; the graceful lines of slender, lancet arches perfectly counterpoint the semi-spherical domes, and every surface is made beautiful with decorated ceramic work, more dazzling in blue than the sober browns of Bukhara. Each ancient monument is a testimony to events, actual or imaginary. One such is the Guri-Emir ('Grave of the Emir') mausoleum,[1] which is especially beautiful with its colourful mosaics, majestic fluted dome covered with blue tiles, and high vaults glittering with gold. Tamerlane, known locally as Timur, and his closest relatives lie buried here. In the centre are four gravestones fenced off on all sides. One of them is very strange – ominously black (the others are of white marble) and of a weird shape. When you look closer, you can see that it is made of dark green nephrite rather than black marble. This is Tamerlane's grave. Many wanted to possess this highly symbolic and precious stone. Nazir Shah even tried to take it away to Persia, but succeeded only in breaking off several pieces. The sarcophagus[2] remained in place – a magnificent and sombre symbol of the vanity of life and eternity of beauty embodied in the precious stone and the perfect lines of the tomb.

The most impressive sight in Samarkand is the famous Registan Square (which means 'Place of Sand'), with its dazzling blue domes and huge madrassahs.[3] On three sides the square is bordered by majestic structures: the Ulughbek madrassah (1417–20), the Sherdor madrassah (1619–36) and the Tillya-Kari madrassah (1647–60). The Ulughbek madrassah originally had fifty dormitory cells housing over a hundred students; the Sherdor ('Bearing Lions') is a mirror image of the Ulughbek. The Tillya-Kari closes Registan Square from the north; its

---

[1] **mausoleum:** large stately tomb
[2] **sarcophagus:** stone or marble coffin
[3] **madrassahs:** educational institutions, particularly for Islamic religious instruction

name means 'Gilded' and, besides being an educational establishment, it also serves as a grand mosque. When we enter this exquisite mosque we find the interior is a blaze of gold. We are told that, when restoration work was being carried out, some of the workmen purposely started a fire so as to steal some of the gold used in the gilding, which they then claimed had been destroyed in the flames. Outside in the courtyard the aesthetic feast continues, and we buy wonderful hand-made ceramic plates and boxes.

My original impressions would be incomplete if we did not visit an open-air bazaar, so we go to a huge, riotous, cacophonously noisy market redolent with the aroma of spices. It is a striking contrast to the beggarly flea-market at the Gostinny Dvor in St Petersburg or the Arbat stalls in Moscow. There, the people seem desperate and nervous, money their only concern, while here they are friendly and happy to bargain. As I walk along the endless counters enjoying the lavish displays of wonderful fruit – sweet grapes, juicy peaches, fragrant melons and purple pomegranates – I feel as though I'm in a museum, feasting my eyes on a magnificent series of still lifes. Suddenly, I hear my name shouted amid the impossible din of the bazaar: 'Makarova! You are Natasha.' I raise my eyes to meet a glittering smile revealing two rows of gold dentures, kind and smiling eyes, and a huge hat in the timeless oriental fashion. This tomato seller remembers me from Leningrad – my fan, he had never missed a single ballet. We met again, some twenty-three years later, in a bazaar in Samarkand. It smacks of a soap opera.

He has no flowers, so he hands me a huge tomato that I start to eat at his counter to please him. I do not ask him how it happens that he, who had trained as an engineer, is selling tomatoes here. He, in turn, doesn't ask me whether I am still on stage. We are glad to meet like two old friends with the past to share.

Next to this bazaar stands the Bibi Khanyam, the grand mosque, decorated with majolica[4] mosaics, carved marble and gilt. The buildings of the main mosque and the two smaller ones were already beginning to crumble in Tamerlane's time. A devastating earthquake in the 1970s did further damage, and it has not yet been restored to its former beauty. The legend goes that Tamerlane's favourite Chinese wife planned the mosque as a gift to her husband on his return from one of his Indian campaigns; but the architect fell in love with her and refused to continue his work unless she agreed to accept his kiss. Eventually she did so and the mosque was completed. When Tamerlane returned, he saw the brand of passion on her cheek – he had the architect tortured and his wife hurled from the highest minaret. From then on, he ordered that all women should wear veils to shield men from the lure of their fatal attractions. With the resurgence of Muslim fundamentalism since the break-up of the Soviet Union, there is implicit irony in the fact that many women are now wearing the veil as an expression of national pride.

---

[4] **majolica:** brightly coloured pottery

Ⓐ *See pages 114–116 for related activities.*

Festival Time in Seville

Jan Morris's travel books are almost better than guide books for the detail they give of the places she visits. In this extract from Spain *she writes of Andalusia and lets us experience something of the famous festival, the Feria of Seville.*

Jan Morris
from *Spain* (1964)

Andalusia gloriously lives up to its reputation, and is as full of colourful vitality as any opera stage; full of hard work, as the labourers pursue their archaic skills in the fields; full of gossip and curiosity and the music of unseen radios, as the cheerful children swarm about your car, and the old ladies in shawls gaze at you unwinking from the doors of their houses. There are no half-measures in such a place, so close to the earth, perilously near the frontiers of caricature. You feel that its people have already made up their minds, after some deliberation: having decided not to cut your throat, for the dramatic effect, they are, with a policeman's salute and a wave from the shrouded grocer, altogether at your service.

Such is romantic Spain at its roots. To see it at its flowering climax, you should go to the famous Feria of Seville, which takes place in April, and is at once so unusual, so entertaining, and so beautiful that few other fairs in the world can match it. The old city warms up to the event for some weeks in advance. The great fairground, down by Carmen's tobacco factory is prettied up with flowers and fairy lamps. The proud families of Andalusia, the clubs, the syndicates, and the livelier commercial firms, erect their tented pavilions along the boulevards. The hotels, cautiously doubling their prices for the occasion, rent out their last upstairs back rooms. The whole rhythm of the city is accelerated, the pressure is intensified, the streets are crowded, the cafés hilarious, magnificent horsemen clatter through the city centre, the stranger feels that some civic blood-vessel is surely about to burst – and finally, early in April, all this happy fever detonates the annual explosion of the Feria.

It is part a parade, of horses, fashions and handsome citizens. It is part a binge, where people eat and drink all night, and dance into the morning. It is part an entertainment, where the best dancers and musicians of Andalusia come to display their talents. It is part a mating session, where the best families gather to share reminiscences, swop prejudices and introduce eligible nephews to likely nieces. In the morning there takes place the most brilliant of all Spain's *paseos* – a *paseo* with horses. Hour after hour, in the warm spring sunshine, the Andalusians ride up and down that fairground – to see and be seen, look each other's dressage up and down, and inquire after the dear Marquis. The married and the very young ride by in lovely polished carriages, drawn sometimes by the proudest of mules, sometimes by pairs of elegant Arabs, and just occasionally by that prodigy of the carriage trade, a five-in-hand. Their coachmen are sometimes decked up in gorgeous liveries, turbans, toppers, Druse costume or tam-o'-shanters, and often some winsome grand-daughter perches herself upon the open hood of the barouche, her frilled white skirt drooping over the back.

As for those of marriageable age, they trot up and down those boulevards like figures of Welsh mythology: two to a horse, the young man proud as a peacock in front, the girl seductively side-saddle behind. He is dressed in all the splendour of the Andalusian dandy, the tightest of jackets and the most rakish of hats, looking lithe, lean and possibly corseted; she wears a rose in her hair and a long, full, flowering, flounced polka-dot dress – blue, pink, mauve, bright yellow or flaming red. Never was there such a morning spectacle. The old people look marvellously well fed and valeted; the coachmen are superbly cocksure;

and sometimes one of those courting couples will wheel around with a spark of hoofs, the beau reining sharply in like a cowboy at the brink of a canyon, the belle clutching his shapely waist or holding the flower in her hair, to mount the pavement to some gay pavilion, the horse snorting and the lovers laughing, and accept a stirrup cup[1] from a smiling friend.

In the evening the binge begins, and the fairground, blazing with flags and lights, becomes a stupendous kind of night club. The air is loud with handclaps and the clicking of castanets,[2] and all among the huge ornamental buildings that flank the fairground, with their ponds, parapets, and courtyards, groups of young people are dancing in the shadows – sometimes suddenly swooping, like so many flocks of chirping birds, from one corner to another, from one alcove to the next, or helter-skelter over a hump-back bridge to the other side of the water. The bright pavilions of the fairground streets now sizzle with celebration – bands thumping, dishes clashing, families deep in gossip over their drinks, gypsies cooking ghastly greasy stews outside tents of sybaritic[3] silkiness, stolid railwaymen listening to the music, or groups of children, resplendent in their southern fineries, dancing stately measures on a stage. Sometimes you hear a hoarse flourish of *cante jondo*, from some gypsy virtuoso[4] hired for the evening. Sometimes the young bloods come dancing by, arm in arm across the pavement, with a transistor to give them rhythm, and feathers in their hats. Everywhere there is the beat of the flamenco,[5] the clatter of heels and castanets, the creak of carriage wheels, the smell of horses, the swish of romantic skirts and the noise, like the shuttle of distant looms, of twenty thousand clapping hands.

---

[1] **stirrup cup:** cup containing an alcoholic drink (offered to a person on a horse)
[2] **castanets:** percussion instrument made from curved pieces of hollow wood
[3] **sybaritic:** luxurious
[4] **virtuoso:** master of musical technique
[5] **flamenco:** Spanish dance

It lasts for most of the night, three nights running, and when you wake up in the morning, to feel the city in a happy but exhausted hush all around you, it is as though the whole experience has only been some elaborate dream – too much red Rioja, perhaps, or eating your mussel soup too fast.

See pages 114–116 for related activities.

Buses, Bikes and Trains

Journeys take on a different nature according to the means of transport taken. Do you take the more energetic and personal way and travel by bicycle? Do you risk the buses, which could range from luxurious people carriers to those that are poorly upholstered and perhaps don't suit your size, or do you go for the speed (usually!) of trains that offer varied degrees of comfort? You could also go on foot or take a boat or a plane but whatever your choice the means of transport has an effect on the style and character of your journey.

Basket Search in Burma

Rory MacLean travelled through Burma in the late 1990s as the country was in the grip of a ruthless military regime. He travelled with his wife, a basket-maker, in search of a very particular basket they had seen in the British Museum storeroom. MacLean had long been fascinated by Burma and this quest gave him what he had been waiting for – a reason for the journey. He was lucky enough to meet Aung San Suu Kyi, the leader of the democratic party elected but not allowed to rule; she is currently under house arrest. The MacLeans decided to travel to Mandalay by bus because, as he recalls, 'We had the freedom to choose.'

Rory MacLean

from *Under the Dragon* (1998)

We could have flown to Mandalay, of course. We could have dropped our knapsack into the thin boy's arms and joined the German couple on the back seat of the minibus to trade stories of plum-size cockroaches and egg-on-sugared-toast hotel breakfasts. We could have confused landscape and historical remains with the living country. Our credit card could have been debited and a round of drinks ordered. Peanuts and crispies would have been served in the departure lounge. We could have checked in, taken off, touched down and still had time to take in Mandalay Hill before lunch at the Novotel. But instead we decided not to luxuriate on the ATR 72–210 *Hintha* Golden Flight. It wasn't a question of saving the cost of the airfare, or even our response to the rumours that the airline had been financed by the profits of arms trading. It was for a greater reason than that. We had the freedom to choose.

The next morning, at the hour when – as the Burmese say – 'one first sees the veins on one's hands', we sat in an Isuzu bus beside the

Irrawaddy, yawning. In the cool dawn a drowsy mother lit her breakfast fire. The match hissed, kindling crackled and her child called out in its sleep. Waking sparrows chattered. The ebony turned to ash grey, tinged itself with rose then burst into morning bloom. Voices warmed in the sun, growing excited with the heat. Our driver detached himself from a circle of conversation and slipped behind the wheel. He was a cut above the usual line-bus driver, wearing a dusty tailored blazer with his *longyi*. His ticket collector sported a flutter of banknotes around his fingers and a T-shirt which read 'Top of the Heap'. The engine shook itself awake and, with an alarming shriek of gears, the bus eased forward along the low, muddy riverbank.

The Irrawaddy rises in the southern Himalayas, winds its way through the Kachin Hills, curls around the rice paddies of the Shan Plateau and crosses the arid central plains before uncoiling, like the frayed end of a rope, into the Andaman Sea. In an earlier age our dashing driver might have captained one of the forty steamers of the Irrawaddy Flotilla Company. At the height of British rule its ships carried nine million passengers a year along the river. But instead of sounding a polished brass whistle, he tooted his horn to encourage a bullock-cart out of our path, and startled a heron fishing in the shallows.

The bus gathered speed, racing along the single-lane carriageway and swaying onto the cinder shoulder to pass oncoming lorries or local pick-ups with live pigs lashed to their roofs. The wild motion shook us with such violence that our vision soon became blurred. Our bodies bounced out of contact with the hard bench seat. Within thirty minutes our brains felt as bruised within the bone of our heads as were we inside the metal box of the bus. The appalling road was a long, weaving Morse-code line of contact and non-contact, and after an hour our comfortable Pagan hotel seemed a lifetime away. A stone punctured the muffler, releasing a deafening blast of exhaust. The wearying movement created an impression of great distances travelled, but after four hours we had covered only forty miles. 'I think I need a new bra,' Katrin groaned as we shivered and jolted in Myingyan, our lunch stop.

The Burmese passengers scrambled out of the bus and into the café to wolf down plates of curry. We took longer to collect ourselves, and were besieged by a clamour of street vendors, balancing on their heads trays of plastic-wrapped quail eggs, bunches of grapes and fierce ruby-red sausages. Katrin ate a tiny boiled egg and I managed to stomach a *samosa*, its fried pastry stuffed with pigeon peas. We drank three bottles of purified water ('UV Treated for your Good Health and Extra Comfort') while our driver finished his second 'brain sweet' bread pudding. Across the road a gang of villagers thatched a house with toddy[1] fronds, and we remembered Ma Swe.

The journey after lunch was no more comfortable, but because the morning had numbed our senses, it became easier to think. I noticed again that, as on the Meiktila line-bus, children slept on their parents' laps undisturbed by the vicious motion. Their calm reminded me of the words of Major Grant Allen, as quoted by Scott in *The Burman*. 'Unlike the generality of Asiatics,' Allen had declared with a Victorian's certainty, 'the Burmese are not a fawning race. They are cheerful, and singularly alive to the ridiculous; buoyant, elastic, soon recovering from personal or domestic disaster.'

Allen's assertion that the Burmese were 'not individually cruel', yet were 'indifferent to the shedding of blood on the part of their rulers' intrigued me. Watching the children, dozing innocents in a harsh environment, I began to wonder if the tolerance of tyranny could be a legacy of the past. Was the present military dictatorship simply a modern version of the old despotic[2] monarchy? If this was the case, then could the 1988 uprising, with all its hoped for democracy, have been no more the result of Western influences than a response to an intrinsic Burmese

---

[1] **toddy:** palm tree
[2] **despotic:** tyrannical

need for freedom? Neither Allen's not Scott's words could explain the central dichotomy[3] of Burma: that the gentle generosity of the people – the constant offers to share food, to give us presents and pay our bus fare – was at odds with the grasping brutality of authority.

Beyond the bus's dust-caked windows the scorched plains gradually yielded to tilled land. Against a backdrop of sunflower fields a goatherd leaned on a bush and lowered juicy new shoots to within his herd's reach. Chalk-white egrets[4] fed in emerald-green rice paddies. Beneath a stern but imperfect red and white sign – 'Anyone who Gets Riotustive and Unruly is our Enemy' – we entered Mandalay on sore, bruised bottoms.

---

[3] **dichotomy:** division into two parts
[4] **egrets:** wading birds

Ⓐ *See pages 117–119 for related activities.*

Seeking Miss Small

Irma Kurtz takes a very different bus journey, a three-month journey around the USA by Greyhound bus. The Greyhounds are famous in the States as they offer a regular and cheap service the length and breadth of that huge country as well as to parts of Canada and Mexico. Irma Kurtz journeys to find her roots and in the extract here she is arriving in Elwood, Indiana, the place where her mother went to school.

Irma Kurtz

from *The Great American Bus Ride* (1993)

BUS 9 to Anderson and Elwood, Indiana

Strictly speaking, buses do not go within thirty miles of Elwood. First, I had to take an American Line bus to Anderson and then, as Elwood has neither bus nor taxi service, I had to arrange to continue in a shared van called the 'Tram' that went everywhere in the country for three dollars, and had to be booked in advance. The Tram did not run on Sundays or public holidays, when Elwood, like much of the state, was effectively closed to anyone without a car. By the time I'd made my travel arrangements and found a locker in which to check my bag, there were barely two hours left to have a look at Indianapolis, and get the feel of it.

My father always complained that the only place on earth more boring than Indianapolis was Elwood, Indiana. I found the city pleasant, however, though rather dozy, and with a tempo much more southern than I had expected. Admittedly, I have a vested interest in Indianapolis: it's where my parents met when they were both at university there. I owe the place a favour, and I'm glad I had a chance to show my appreciation.

'Well done,' said a passerby. He looked like a CPA[1] or a bank official. I had been photographing some noteworthy art-deco interior design and

---

[1] **CPA:** certified public accountant

he had seen me go out of my way to drop a film wrapper in a public receptacle. 'You're a good citizen. We need more like you in Indianapolis.'

The single aspect of Indiana my father never mocked or criticised was the countryside, and looking out of the bus at the gentle land spread with thickets and streams, it was easy to see why long walks had been the basis of my parents' courtship. My mother was charmed by my father's past in New York, and by his family's memories of Eastern Europe, which in many places has the same made-for-summer, windswept look of Indiana. The stories Mother liked best to tell and write derived from my father's childhood instead of her own. But for me, it was different: I sometimes felt that I knew my father's past to a point further back than he himself remembered. It was all familiar to me and bred in my dreams. My mother's roots, on the other hand, out of Elwood, Indiana, were as alien as they could be. Mr Longerbone, the grocer; Mr Sneed, who kept the drugstore; Elbert Cotton, Mr Cute, and Mr Snodgrass; 'King' Leeson, who founded the department store on Main Street, and his daughter, 'Missy': what names were those? They had a Yankee Doodle ring, too blue-eyed to be believed, and utterly foreign to me.

When my mother was barely seven, her father died of TB[2] in Denver, and her vain, pretty, stupid mother, my Grandma Annie, who was herself only a child, came back to live with her parents in Elwood. They were a displaced and moody couple with big problems of their own. In my mind's eye, they are all dark figures while the other Elwood folks are pale as bedclothes, windblown through empty streets. My mother I see as a vivid child among them, and so are her chums, the offspring of a few Syrian families, as ill-placed as Jews in Elwood. A pair of Syrian brothers who used to hang on every word of my little mother's made-up tales of ghosts and the headless dead were the dazzling Zemurod and Osman.

---

[2] **TB:** tuberculosis

They left town as soon as they were grown, and then came back not very long afterward to open a whorehouse down the road. It prospered, too. Those Elwood kids had a serious gift for vengeance.

The Tram was waiting for me when my bus pulled into Anderson. As we rode to Elwood, I held the image of a little hotel in the middle of Main Street, with aspidistras[3] in the lobby, and in its bathrooms big tubs on lions' feet. There was bound to be an oaken bar too, where travelling salesmen in flashy suits stood each other cold beers and compared notes on local trade. But Elwood, though left behind indeed by time, as must be countless American towns where Greyhound doesn't stop, had not been left intact. Anyhow, men travelling in ladies' underwear, and notions,[4] and dry goods, are probably no more to be found on the back roads. And the only accommodation for visitors turned out to be two motels face-to-face across a highway about three miles before Elwood could be said properly to begin. One of them was open for business, but I asked the driver of the Tram to drop me off at the other; I couldn't have said why, unless it was the lazy look of the scrawled sign on the door, 'Back in 5 mins,' that put me in mind of Hoagy Carmichael.[5]

Big clouds were rolling in from the horizon, racing against night, and already rain fell in streaks on nearby fields. I could barely make out the words 'Welcome to Elwood' on a sign at the corner where the highway met the road that led straight into town. Only the big *M* of a McDonald's nearby hung on to the remaining sunlight and contrived to turn the whole scene into an ad for fast food. At last, the proprietor drove up in a noisy old car. He looked surprised to see a customer, and in a slightly bemused way he opened his office and waved me inside. He was in his early sixties, a local man, born and bred in Elwood. He told me 'King' Leeson's daughter 'Missy' was still alive, though well into her eighties,

---

[3] **aspidistras:** plants with long tough green leaves
[4] **notions:** materials for sewing (for example pins, cotton, ribbon)
[5] **Hoagy Carmichael:** an American pianist, singer and composer

and had only a little while earlier given up managing the family store. Oh, yes, the old place was still there, though the rumour was it would soon be turned into a public library. I couldn't miss it when I went into town next day. Fancy someone coming from so far away who knew about Leeson's and old Mr Longerbone.

'What was your mother's name?' he asked as we walked to the chalet I'd rented in a row of ten.

'Her name was Auerbach,' I said. 'But after her father died and they came back here, she was probably known by her mother's family name.'

'And that was?'

Big raindrops were splattering the path around us and forming instantaneous puddles.

'My grandmother's family name?' I felt a queer reluctance to tell him, almost shame. 'The name was Kessler.'

'Ah, I see,' he said. 'Yes. Kessler. Oh, yes. I don't recall folks by that name myself. But I don't suppose your mother's memories of Elwood are very happy.'

In the 1920s, when Wendell Willkie spent a few days back home in Elwood, he was feted all over town, but his driver had to find lodgings somewhere else, because he was black. Back then, when Mother was a girl, the KKK[6] ran Elwood and most of the state. Now on the fence at the town limits are welcoming plaques from the Kiwanis club, the Optimists, the Lions, the Veterans of Foreign Wars and a couple of local churches. The Klan is no longer represented. Although I'm sure the Moose, and Elks, and Optimists, and Knights of Pythias, and Masons, and women of the Moose, and Elks, et cetera, do fine things for some of the community, the evident taste for secret societies throughout Middle America gave me the whim-whams, and no place more than in Elwood, Indiana, where,

---

[6] **KKK:** Ku Klux Klan (secret racist organisation formed in the southern states of America after the US Civil War)

how well Mother remembers, the KKK used to march regularly down Main Street. Sometimes the morning afterward she'd find their obscenities scribbled on the front gate.

Early next morning I accepted a lift from my host to the main cemetery on the opposite side of town from his motel, a trip of four or five miles. No sooner had his car rattled away and left me than the skies, which had been swollen since dawn, broke open and let fall a deluge of rain set to wash Elwood off the face of the earth. With the cape of my blessed Driza Bone[7] converted into a hood, I fled past headstones and mausoleums to a small office building at the far side from the entrance. The door was locked and there was no sign of anyone behind the streaming windows. A big open-sided shed leaned against one wall, and I made for it fast. Two men were already sheltering in there. One of them was wearing a suit and had probably come to pay his respects at a grave. The other was dressed in working clothes; I took him to be a grounds keeper. They were both in their late fifties and clean shaven. The businessman had a glum, clever Hoosier face. The other fellow was fat and jowly. They nodded my way and went on with their conversation.

'Now, I'm one of those guys, I always talk over what I'm gonna do with the wife before I do it,' the big man said. 'Been married thirty-two years. That's why there's so much darned dee-vorce these days. He does what he wants. She does what she wants.'

'Used to be,' said the other man, 'trends came from the East. Now they appear to be coming in mostly from California.'

'Anyways they come, Indiana's in the middle … '

'Drugs … '

'Dee-vorce … '

We stood in a row, me a little behind the men, looking out at the rain falling on stones and bare trees.

---

[7] **Driza Bone:** all-weather coat

'Ever wonder,' said the man in the suit after a while, 'how come no good trends ever seem to come our way?'

'If I was young ... ,' said the big guy.

'... I'd get out,' the other one said.

The office of Elwood's main cemetery could be put as is into a provincial museum to show what offices were like at the turn of the century. Against the back wall was a big safe, black and rimmed in gold leaf. It was set on wheels. Deadly spindles on the ancient desk were onion-packed with papers, and the telephone was an upstanding prototype of its kind. In summer, flypaper strips are tacked to the dark beams overhead, I'll bet, and the ancient fan inside a cage of chicken wire is no doubt switched on to blow the dust around.

'Her name was Small, you say?' the old fellow asked. He'd shuffled through first one cedarwood box, then another, full of yellowing cards covered in cellophane. 'What was her first name, do you know?'

'I'm afraid not. She was my mother's teacher a long, long time ago.'

Wheezing and bent, he reached down a huge leather-bound book from the top of a filing cabinet. For a long time he turned pages where I saw names once written in black, now faded and coppery. After a lot of dry, rustling pages and drip, drip, drip from outside where the trees were shaking off rain, he stopped with his finger on a name. He turned the book so I could read the entry. Mary Small had been born in 1873 and died in 1940.

'She's the only female Small interred in this here graveyard,' he said. 'She's gotta be the one.'

'To be a good American,' Miss Small announced to her fourth-grade civics class, 'a person's got to be Protestant, white, and born here.' Whereupon she'd whirled around and pointed at my mother and said, 'Minnie Auerbach, you wipe that grin off your face!'

Thus, seventy-odd years later, I stood at the foot of the former teacher's grave, with the mud sucking at my heels, and, pointing to the headstone, I said aloud: 'Miss Mary Small, Minnie's girl has come all this way to tell you, wipe that grin off your face!'

No sooner had the words left my mouth than the downpour began again.

It was a good few miles to walk in the damp twilight past empty shops and derelict houses, some of them big and one splendid, until I came back to the major crossroads and the pseudocivilisation of McDonald's, Arby's and Captain Bob's Catfish. As soon as I was in my room, I telephoned Mother. She was already in Southern California, where she prefers to spend the winter months near my brother and his family.

'Well, honey, here I am in Elwood. And I have to tell you, the place is half dead.'

'May the other half not linger,' said my mother.

'I remembered the story you used to tell about your civics class. And do you know what I did? I went out to the cemetery and found the grave of your Miss Small. And I told her from you to wipe that grin off her face.'

There was a tiny pause.

'Well, that was a very nice thought, Irm,' my mother said. 'And I don't suppose it makes any difference, seeing as it's all in a good cause. But that teacher I used to tell you about? Her name was Little.'

🅐 *See pages 117–119 for related activities.*

An Unusual Proposal

Stanley Stewart travelled to China on the Trans-Siberian Express from Moscow to journey across the great plains, mountain ranges and deserts, beyond the Great Wall of China to the little-known heart of Asia. His journey is full of incident, not least this unusual proposal of marriage.

Stanley Stewart
from *Frontiers of Heaven* (1995)

So arcane is the process of purchasing train tickets in China that many Chinese depend on *guanxi*, the well-developed network of contacts, friends and family, through which so much is secured in China, from a job to a wife. Only the poor, the hopelessly unconnected, and the foreign are to be found queuing in the booking office, pathetic mugs who don't know any better.

Train tickets are the Chinese Holy Grail and their acquisition has a religious flavour. The ticket windows mimic the confessional with wooden doors shooting open and shut over small dark screens. With the windows placed at waist height, you are obliged either to bow or kneel as you approach. The supplicant posture, the air of mystery, the adherence to ritual and the correct form of words, the belief that the shadowy figure beyond the screen might intercede, might grant absolution, if one could only find the right formula – the whole heady mix is Catholicism at its most obscure.

The scene in the Wuwei train station was depressingly familiar. A cobwebbed queue of petitioners stood before two closed ticket windows. I settled down to wait. Someone handed round a flask of tea.

When I eventually reached the window, and made my request for a ticket to Jiuquan for the following day, I was met by the squeak of rejection familiar to any visitor to China. '*Meiyou*,' she said, without lifting her head.

Meiyou is the eternal negative. It chimes through Chinese days marking shortages, red tape and laziness.

I asked about the next day. '*Meiyou.*' And the day after. '*Meiyou.*' I asked about the next week. '*Meiyou.*' The next month. '*Meiyou.*' I became insistent, asking for a ticket for Jiuquan on any day within the next ten years. The little door slammed shut.

I returned three days running to be met with the same denials. Trains came through Wuwei every day heading west to Jiuquan and points beyond but, if the ticket office could be believed, they arrived and departed full. There were no tickets, ever.

At my hotel I offered the staff large sums of money to procure tickets by fair means or foul. I promised to bribe whoever needed bribing. But they only shook their heads sadly. There were some things that even money could not buy.

I decided to try to get arrested so the authorities would run me out of town. Camera in hand, I went in search of military subjects. I photographed two army jeeps in the main street. I photographed the railway station, a bridge, the court-house, the gaol and the Public Security Bureau headquarters. I photographed the radio mast from three different angles. I had enough stuff for a full-scale invasion, but no one took any notice. Finally I went back to my hotel and photographed the army officers lounging in the lobby. Far from protesting, they posed happily for a group portrait and invited me to dinner. I refused on the grounds that I was a Russian spy. They laughed heartily and slapped me on the back.

The next day I played my final card. I went back to the railway station, and asked the clerk to marry me.

'Where to?' she asked.

'Nowhere. I am asking you to marry me,' I said.

She looked up, a minor triumph in itself. I could see her struggling for words but even '*meiyou*' would not come.

'I want you to marry me.' I spoke loudly. I sensed an audience would be useful. The queue awoke and pressed forward, intrigued by this novel approach. I could see other staff emerging from back rooms. This was something more than a weekend return to Lanzhou.

'I can't get out of this town so I have decided to settle here. You are the only woman I know. I want you to be my wife.'

The stationmaster had arrived, hitherto a reclusive figure.

'Sir,' I said, warming to my role, 'I wish to ask for the hand of one of your employees.' I had spent the previous evening swotting up my Chinese, abandoning the chapter entitled 'At the Railway Station' for the higher ground of 'Visiting friends' and 'Formalities'.

Called from his nap, the stationmaster was dishevelled and confused. Had he been more alert he might have adopted the usual procedure of closing the ticket window. Still bleary from sleep he faltered, and asked me what the problem was.

'I cannot buy a ticket,' I cried. 'So I must have a wife.'

Behind me the queue, astonished to find the stationmaster among them, were growing agitated. In a moment they would all be wanting wives.

Marriage proposals have a way of concentrating minds. The stationmaster and the clerks retreated into the back room. A moment later my prospective fiancée reappeared and shoved a ticket to Jiuquan through the hatch before slamming it shut. I lifted it like a trophy. The queue gazed at me dumbstruck then broke into a little ripple of applause. Faith was a fine thing, and theirs had been reborn.

🅐 *See pages 117–119 for related activities.*

The Highest Railway in the World

Paul Theroux's train journey from his home in Boston, USA, down to Patagonia at the very tip of South America involved travelling on the highest railway in the world. Here he sets off from Lima, Peru, for this, perhaps the toughest part of his long trip.

Paul Theroux
from *The Old Patagonian Express* (1979)

16 The Tren de la Sierra

I left Lima on the train to Huancayo the first chance I got. After arriving at that railhead in the mountains I would make my way by road via Ayacucho to Cuzco and there begin my long descent through Bolivia and Argentina to the end of the line in Patagonia. It was a hasty plan, but how could I know that in three days I would be back in Lima trying to find another route to Cuzco?

The Rimac river flowed past the railway station. At seven in the morning it was black; it became grey as the sun moved above the foothills of the Andes. The sandy mountains at the city's edge gave Lima the feel of a desert city hemmed-in on one side by hot plateaux.[1] It is only a few miles from the Pacific Ocean, but the land is too flat to permit a view of the sea, and there are no sea breezes in the day-time. It seldom rains in Lima. If it did, the huts – several thousand of them – in the shanty town on the bank of the Rimac would need roofs. The slum is odd in another way; besides being entirely roofless, the huts in this (to use the Peruvian euphemism) 'young village' are woven from straw and split bamboo and cane. They are small frail baskets, open to the stars and the sun, and planted beside the river which, some miles from the station, is cocoa-coloured. The people wash in this river water; they drink it and

---

[1] **plateaux:** wide, mainly level areas of elevated land

cook with it; and when their dogs die, or there are chickens' entrails to dispose of, the river receives this refuse.

'Not that they eat chickens very often,' explained the Peruvian in the train. The river, he said, was their life-line and their sewer.

Travelling across this plain it is not immediately apparent how any penetration can possibly be made into the escarpment[2] at the far end – it seems too steep, too bare, too high; the valleys are no more than vertical cracks and there is no evidence of trees or men anywhere in these mountains. They have been burned clean of vegetation and have the soft bulge of naked rock. For twenty-five miles the mountain walls remain in the distance; the train seems deceptively quick, rolling along the river, and then at Chosica it stops. It resumes after five minutes, but never again on the trip does it regain that first burst of speed.

We entered the valley and zig-zagged on the walls. It was hardly a valley. It was a cut in the rock, a slash so narrow that the diesel's hooter hardly echoed: the walls were too close to sustain an answering sound. We were due at Huancayo at four o'clock; by mid-morning I thought we might arrive early, but at noon our progress had been so slow I wondered whether we would get to Huancayo that day. And long before Ticlio I had intimations of altitude sickness. I was not alone; a number of other passengers, some of them Indians, looked distinctly ghastly.

It begins as dizziness and a slight headache. I had been standing by the door inhaling the cool air of these shady ledges. Feeling wobbly, I sat down, and if the train had not been full I would have lain across the seat. After an hour I was perspiring and, although I had not stirred from my seat, I was short of breath. The evaporation of this sweat in the dry air gave me a sickening chill. The other passengers were limp, their heads bobbed, no one spoke, no one ate. I dug some aspirin out of my suitcase and chewed them, but only felt queasier; and my headache did not

---

[2] **escarpment:** long continuous steep face of a plateau caused by erosion

abate. The worst thing about feeling so ill in transit is that you know that if something goes wrong with the train – a derailment or a crash – you will be too weak to save yourself. I had a more horrible thought: we were perhaps a third of the way to Huancayo, but Huancayo was higher than this. I dreaded to think what I would feel like at that altitude.

I considered getting off the train at Matucana, but there was nothing at Matucana – a few goats and some Indians and tin-roofed shacks on the stony ground. None of the stops contained anything that looked like relief or refuge. But this altitude sickness had another punishing aspect: it ruined what could have been a trip of astonishing beauty. I had never seen cliffs like these or been on a railway quite so spectacular ... why was it, in this landscape of such unbelievable loveliness, that I felt as sick as a dog? If only I had the strength to concentrate – I would have been dazzled; but, as it was, the beauty became an extraordinary annoyance.

The pale rose-coloured mountains had the dark stripes and mottled marks of the shells of the most delicate snails. To be ill among them, to be slumped in my seat watching the reddish gravel slides stilled in the crevasses, and the configuration of cliff-faces changing with each change in altitude, was torture so acute that I began to associate the very beautiful with the very painful. These pretty heights were the cause of my sickness. And now my teeth hurt, one molar in particular began to ache as if the nerve had caught fire. I did not know then how a cavity in a bad tooth becomes sore at a high altitude. The air in this blocked hole expands and creates pressure on the nerve, and it is agony. The dentist who told me this had been in the air force. Once, in a sharply descending plane, the cockpit became depressurised and an airman, the navigator, screamed in pain and then one of his teeth exploded.

Some of the train passengers had begun to vomit. They did it in the pitiful unembarrassed way that people do when they are helplessly ill. They puked on the floor, and they puked out of the windows and they made my own nausea greater. Some, I noticed, were staggering though the cars. I thought they were looking for a place to puke, but they returned with balloons. *Balloons?* Then they sat and held their noses and breathed the air from the balloon nozzle.

I stood unsteadily and made for the rear of the train, where I found a Peruvian in a smock filling balloons from a tank of oxygen. He handed these out to distressed-looking passengers who gratefully gulped from them. I took my place in the queue and discovered that a few whiffs of oxygen made my head clear and helped my breathing.

There was a boy in this oxygen car. He had an oxygen balloon, too, and wore a handsome cowboy hat decorated with a band of Inca poker-work.

'If I had thought it was going to be anything like this,' he said, 'I would never have come.'

'You took the words out of my mouth.'

'This oxygen's an improvement. Boy, do I feel shitty.'

We sipped from our balloons.

'You from the States?'

'Massachusetts,' I said.

'I'm from Minnesota. Been in Lima long?'

'One day,' I said.

'It's not that bad,' he said. 'I was there a month. It's one of the cheapest places in South America. They say Cuzco's even cheaper. I figure I'll spend a month or so there, then go back to Lima – get a job on a ship.' He looked at me. 'You're smart to have those warm clothes. I wish I had a jacket like that. All I have is these Lima things. I'll buy a sweater when we get to Huancayo – they make them there. You can get alpaca ones for practically nothing. Jesus, do I feel shitty.'

We entered a tunnel. We had been through other tunnels, but this one was long, and it had a certain distinction: it was at 15,848 feet, the highest railway tunnel in the world. The train was loud – deafening, in fact, and I don't think I had ever felt sicker in my life. I sprayed the last of my balloon gas into my mouth, swallowed, and got another one. 'I feel like throwing up,' said the fellow from Minnesota. In the weak yellow light, with his cowboy hat over his eyes, he looked limp and fatally stricken. I did not feel so well myself, but when we emerged from the Galera Tunnel I knew we were past the highest point, and having survived that I was sure I would make it to Huancayo.

'This ship,' I said. 'The one you're going to get a job on. Where do you plan to go?'

'Home,' he said. 'I'll get one to the States. If I'm lucky I'll be back the end of April. I really want to see Minneapolis in the spring.'

'Is it as pretty as this?'

'It's better than this.'

We were now high enough to be able to see across the Andes, the whole range of mountains which, on some curves, were visible for hundreds of miles. They are not solitary peaks, but rather closely packed summits which, surprisingly, grow lighter as the distance deepens. I asked the Minnesotan how he planned to get to Cuzco. He had been in Lima for a month; his information would be good, I thought. He said there was a bus and if I was interested we could take it together. It didn't cost much, but he had heard it sometimes took four or five days to reach Cuzco. It depended on the road. This was the rainy season: the road through Ayacucho would be bad.

At La Oroya, where the line branches – the other line goes north to the tin and copper mines of Cerro de Pasco – our train was delayed. La Oroya itself was desolate and cold. Children came to the platform to beg, and sacks were loaded. Walking made my throat burn, so I sat and wondered whether I should eat anything. There were Indians selling knitted goods – mufflers and ponchos – also fried cakes and burned bits of meat. I drank a cup of sour tea and took some more aspirin. I was rather eager to get back on the train, so that I could get another balloon of oxygen.

When we boarded, an old Indian woman stumbled on the platform.

She had three bundles – cloth, packets of greasy newspaper, a kerosene lamp. I helped her up. She thanked me and told me in Spanish that she was going to Huancavelica, some miles beyond Huancayo. 'And where are you going?'

I told her, and then I asked her if the people here spoke Quechua, the Inca language.

'Yes,' she said. 'That is my language. Everyone speaks Quechua here. You will see in Cuzco.'

We crawled the rest of the afternoon towards Huancayo, and the longer we went the more I marvelled at the achievement of this mountain railway. It is commonly thought that it was planned by American Henry Meiggs, but it was actually a Peruvian, Ernesto Malinowski, who surveyed the route; Meiggs supervised and promoted it, from its beginning in 1870 until his death in 1877. But it was another twenty years before the railway reached Huancayo. A trans-Andean line, from Huancayo to Cuzco, although proposed and surveyed in 1907, had never been built. If it had been, my arrival at the muddy mountain town would have been more hopeful; as it was, I felt too sick to eat, too dazed to go on or do anything but lie shivering in bed, still wearing my leather jacket, reading the poems and devotions of John Donne. It was comfortless stuff for a cold night in the Andes: 'As sickness is the greatest misery, so the greatest misery of sickness is solitude; when the infectiousness of the disease deters them who should assist from coming; even the physician dares scarce come. Solitude is a torment which is not threatened in hell itself.'

A *See pages 117–119 for related activities.*

Bicycle Buying in Hungary

In 1990, just after the fall of Communism and of Rumania's ruthless leader Nicolae Ceauşescu and his wife, Elena, Dervla Murphy, an intrepid Irish traveller, set out to trek and 'to share in Rumania's happiness'. She was rather accident-prone and ended up making several visits. The final one was by way of Hungary where she decided to buy a bicycle.

Dervla Murphy
from *Transylvania and Beyond* (1992)

No one had warned me that it takes ten days, at least, to buy a Russian bicycle in Budapest: though this may be reduced to five days should you happen to have a celebrated Hungarian friend who can put in a passionate plea on your behalf.

First you find your bicycle, which is easy. Soon I saw what I wanted, hanging high in the window of a vast city-centre state store called Szivarvany. Model 153–421 was conspicuously marked 4,800 forints, then approximately $60. All the non-Soviet models cost at least 20,000 forints, an out-of-the-question investment since this machine was to be left with a Rumanian friend. Inside, hundreds of 153–421s were stacked along one wall in an alarmingly unassembled state; one would need an honours degree in engineering to get them on the road. In sign language I pleaded with a grumpy, undersized young man to sell me the assembled display model. He responded, naturally enough, in Hungarian, which language isolates its users to a unique extent from their fellow-Europeans. Yet his expression and tone conveyed a clear message: in this unreformed state store no rule could possibly be bent for the sake of a mere customer. Despairingly I sought an English-speaker, or even a German- or French-speaker. In any Rumanian city multi-linguists would at once have swarmed, excitedly eager to help the foreigner. In Budapest it is otherwise.

Next I tried to coax the young man into himself assembling a bicycle for me. He looked scandalised and dismissed the notion with a series of graphic gestures. Then he handed me a large twenty-four-page booklet in Russian, amply illustrated with twenty-six diagrams; the first showed a naked man standing beside my bicycle-to-be, measuring his legs against the wheels. Now came *my* graphic gestures, conveying horror and despair. The young man shrugged impatiently and produced a formidable document – five foolscap[1] pages, hideously resembling an income tax return form. Presenting me with this sheaf, his manner suggested that now my problem was solved.

Page one was headed, in capitals: ELVESZETT JOTALLASI JEGYET CSAK AZ ELADAS NAPJANAK HITELT ERDEMLO IGAZOLASA (pl. DATUMMAL ES BELYEGZOVEL ELLATOTT SZAMLA, ELADASI JEGYZEK) ESETEN POTPLUNK! I wondered if the exclamation mark indicated that this was vital information needing at once to be absorbed by potential buyers of model 153–421.

Briskly the young man turned to another page, borrowed a pen and underlined VALLALAT BELYEGZOJE and ADOIGAZGATASI AZONOSITOSZAMA. I looked at him reproachfully, then took out my Angol–Magyar, Magyar–Angol *utiszotar*. It listed none of those words; the nearest was *azonos* ('identical') which shed no light on anything. At last the young man smiled; Hungarians appreciate, as well they might, even the feeblest of efforts to cope with their language. He then noticed a street plan in my shirt pocket. Spreading it on the counter, he indicated Egressy ut., wrote '17–21' in the margin, then turned to another page of the sheaf and there underlined *XIV Egressy ut., 17–21*. Semi-hysterically I giggled as the filler dropped. Of course! My purchase must be taken, with the sheaf, booklet and my receipt, to an establishment on the far side of Pest where some genius would assemble it. Mine was not to reason why, mine but to do or die (almost) while wheeling model 153–421 through Budapest's traffic.

---

[1] **foolscap:** 13^{1}/2 inches by 17 inches (33.75cm by 42.5cm)

That however, was tomorrow's challenge; it was then too late to seek Egressy ut. So model 153–421 spent the night on the first-floor balcony of my friend's flat; he was light enough, I noted with relief, to be easily carried upstairs – an important attribute, since many Rumanian blocs are liftless.

My three-mile walk to Egressy ut. was memorable. Hungarians tend to use Budapest's long wide straight streets as racing-tracks; seventy miles per hour is acceptable, which in a city indicates some sort of mass death-wish. Even the trams and trolley-buses compete at lethal speeds, swaying along as though drunk, while the metro elevators whizz up and down like something in a cartoon film. To the unnerved visitor, it seems that Budapest's drivers display all the most unpleasant Hungarian qualities: aggression, ruthlessness, self-centredness. On my first day in the city, a young woman carrying a toddler was knocked down beside me when using a zebra crossing while the green light was on; a car swooped round the corner, ignoring the lights as too many Hungarian drivers do, and the victim had to be taken to hospital with a broken leg and a concussed child. The driver fled the scene but I was assured he would almost certainly be caught, through co-operation between public and police. My own leg might have been broken *en route* to Egressy ut. when a car parked by the pavement abruptly reversed with never a backward glance; I leaped to safety just in time.

No. 17–21 Egressy ut. was a strange left-over from the Communist era – at least I hope it was strange, not the sort of establishment Hungarians still have to combat on a daily basis. In a dreary barn-sized office men and women sat at metal desks, surrounded by tightly-packed filing cabinets, behind a bisecting counter. They looked pallid and embittered – as would we all, given such a work-place. On the public's side of the counter the queue occupied sagging plastic-covered settees. Their problems were, it seemed, car-related, and for fifty minutes I watched men (only men) with furrowed brows laboriously filling in multi-paged documents which were then – often after much argument – lavishly rubber-stamped and filed away. How, I wondered, was I going to negotiate those bureaucratic shoals *sans* interpreter? But in fact the sheaf from Szivarvany, plus model 153–421, needed no verbal input from me. An elderly woman clerk, with glinting purple-copper hair such as one used to see on celluloid dolls, simply indicated where I was to sign another document guaranteeing that I could collect my property ten days hence.

I stared, appalled, at this rubber-stamped date – then smiled ingratiatingly at the woman and boldly wrote in another, three days hence. The woman ground her teeth and struck out my date. Ten days or nothing, her expression said. And there was no charge; assembly was free and she wasn't interested in (or didn't understand?) my clumsy wordless hinting at a bribe. A dungaree-clad man then materialised at my elbow and wheeled model 153–421 away, beckoning me to follow. Scepticism took over when I saw my purchase joining hundreds – yes, *hundreds* – of unassembled clones. *Ten days?* More likely a month! I filled in the label presented by Dungarees, tied it to the handlebars as requested, was given yet another document – to be shown prior to collection – and went on my way, sorrowfully.

My host, however, was not so easily cowed by the esoteric[2] bicycle-buying rituals of his native city. Next morning he accompanied me to Egressy ut., where I was promoted to being a famous Irish writer who *had* to leave Budapest three days hence and could *not* leave without her bicycle.

Three days later, at the appointed hour – 11 am precisely – a meticulously assembled model 153–421 was secured to the roof of my friend's car and eventually we were dropped off at Nyiregyhaza, some forty miles from the Rumanian border. Naming model 153–421 was easy; he had to be 'Luke', in honour of my celebrated Hungarian friend, John Lukacs.

---

[2] **esoteric:** difficult to understand

Cyclists bring out the worst in status-conscious Rumanians. If in middle age you can afford only a bicycle, and are tanned Gypsy brown and shabbily dressed, you must be a total failure and are likely to be treated as such – not of course in the villages, but in tourist hotels or even shoddy urban cafés and restaurants. (Methods of transport are graded thus on the status scale: motor cars, motor vans, horse-carts, ox-carts, bicycles, donkey-carts.) As most tourist hotels excluded Luke, I sometimes had to sit shivering outside in the wind and rain while waiting for the local with whom I had an appointment. I could have left Luke locked, but that would not have deterred fiddling small boys from possibly doing irreparable damage to his delicate gears.

Apart from this easily endured loss of status, Rumania provides excellent cycling territory. There are only a few snags; broken glass; worn-out concrete roads; new concrete roads; Austro-Hungarian pavé roads; main roads (so described on the map) that prove to be uncycleable tracks; hot liquid tar; temporarily (I hope) debilitating agricultural sprays; anti-cyclist truck drivers in urban areas and – the only serious problem – sheepdogs trained to kill intruders in rural areas.

The broken glass sets up a conflict between self-preservation and tyre-preservation; oddly enough, the latter instinct dominates in a country where tyres cannot be replaced. For some reason, perhaps understood by psychologists, the breaking of glass obviously relieves the inner tensions of millions of Rumanians. How else explain the shimmering proliferation of broken bottles by the wayside on every main road? To avoid this hazard cyclists must suddenly veer out from the verge and only good fortune protects one from the traffic up behind.

Worn-out concrete roads may sound like a mere triviality but they don't *feel* so as one judders over miles of large uneven stones that have outlasted the concrete. Even new concrete roads have blocks so ill-aligned that every five yards there is a violent bump, and the regularity of this unpleasant sensation become peculiarly irritating. The pavé roads are something else again; where these have emerged from under the post-Trianon Rumanian roads they remain as good as new, a memorial to the efficiency of the Magyar administration but a literal pain in the arse for cyclists. A few such roads, designed for horse-traffic only, are now being used by heavy trucks but show no sign of disintegrating. These are hand-built works of art, rather than engineering feats.

The long-since-defunct main roads are no threat to cyclists, but some bridges have so drastically wasted away that a motor car would inevitably end up in the river for lack of warning signs.

Hot liquid tar is a common hazard in springtime, when main roads are being 'repaired' by work-forces of astounding laziness and incompetence. An excess of boiling, too-thin tar is slopped into pot-holes, topped with a shovelful of chips and left to stream over the rest of the surface – a tyre-endangering menace. One has no choice but to get off that road, not always easy or safe on a mountainside. An alternative form of incompetence is to pile mounds of chips into mega-pot-holes, thus unwittingly creating the sort of traffic-slowing obstacles known in other countries as 'ramps'.

My most memorable encounter with poisonous spray happened near Tirgu Neamt, where the occupants of three stationary Gypsy wagons frantically signalled me to stop; they had the air of people waiting at a level-crossing barrier. Foolishly I pedalled on, having been so often warned against Gypsy hold-ups, and soon I had reason to regret my mistrust. A biplane was spraying the whole area and after a few miles I could scarcely breathe and had to dismount – dizzy and nauseated, with a pounding heart. Slowly I continued, wheeling Luke, and on at last emerging from that zone saw another queue of carts – both Gypsies' and villagers'. This was my only experience of aerial spraying; usually giant tanks lumber over the fields, discharging their lethal load to the detriment of the local wildlife. Near Gheorgheni, where intensive spraying had a dire effect on my eyes and throat, several swallows collided with me, then dropped to the ground. I stopped to examine them; they were not yet dead, but stunned and gasping oddly.

Rumania's truck-drivers relieve their boredom by gambling with cyclists' lives. Habitually their juggernauts roared past within inches of me and a grinning passenger always stared back to observe whether or not I had survived.

And then there are the sheepdogs, a major threat to cyclists between the Balkans and the Khyber Pass; but more of them anon.

Ⓐ *See pages 117–119 for related activities.*

Chinese Bicycle Torture

Getting a bicycle proved hard enough for Dervla Murphy – for this anonymous traveller who entered a travel writing competition, holding on to one was even more of a challenge.

Anon
from *Travellers' Tales from Heaven and Hell* (1997)

I hired a bicycle from the little shop outside my hostel with the few Yuan[1] I had left in cash, so I could bicycle to the Bank of China on the far side of the city. The friendly rental guy had wanted a deposit for his precious vehicle (bike thefts comprise most of the crime rate in China) and for this he wanted hard cash. On any other day this would have been fine but today just happened to be the day when I needed to change my US Dollars into local currency, hence my trip to the bank and the requiring of the bike. The irony of the situation was apparent, but just as I began to resign myself to the long wet walk, he pointed out that he also accepted passports as deposits. This is a common thing to do in hotels, both in Asia and Europe, to ensure that you pay your bill, but in this case I had my doubts. I had heard stories from fellow travellers of people locking their hired bikes up somewhere, only to find that they had gone when they returned to them later – the bikes having been liberated by their owner with a spare key! I was far less willing to risk my passport than cash in such a scam, but luckily I had my own lock and chain, so reluctantly handed the document over and headed off into the pouring rain.

I was pleased not to have been killed by the hoards of cyclists who, along with the drivers of the occasional motor vehicle, seem to choose to ignore any rules at junctions. However my good mood, which increased upon finding my bike where I had left it when returning from the bank,

---

[1] **Yuan:** Chinese currency

suddenly changed when I found it with 'added security'. I could not believe what I was seeing and it took me several useless tugs at the chain to fully accept the predicament. My first solution to the problem admittedly did not rank on the all time top ten of brilliant solutions! Noticing that the post was fixed into a concrete base, I wondered if I could carry the whole affair back to the hostel, and present it to the rental man to sort out.

Suddenly a man popped out from goodness knows where and began to make suggestions. After a lot of futile exchanged words and gestures, it gradually became clear that he was telling me to look for a man with a pointy hat. It dawned on me that this mysterious clue meant the ancient-looking policeman, who had begun to hover behind my new found friend. He was less willing than my friend to try and communicate. After what seemed like an eternity, it transpired I had been given my first ever parking ticket – the chain being the equivalent of a wheel clamp!

In the end I had no choice but to pay the fine, but not before learning a moral to this story which is not, as you might expect, never to let your passport out of your sight, but rather this: Never lock your bicycle to a handy post if the sign that it bears transpires to translate as 'No Parking!'

Ⓐ *See pages 117–119 for related activities.*

Water!

It is amazing how often water, or the lack of it, plays a part in a journey. Lack of it causes huge problems and too much of it can be tricky too. Its place in the environment is central, and rivers, and lakes and seas offer beauty and adventure – who can ever forget the perfect sunset reflected on rippling water?

Underwater, Down Under

Travelling in Australia, Bill Bryson often worries about the lack of water but in this extract there is rather too much of it for his taste!

Bill Bryson
from *Down Under* (2000)

In the morning, the rain had stopped but the skies were dark and dirty and the sea full of chop. Just looking at it made me feel faintly ill. I am not enamoured of the ocean or anything within it, and the prospect of bouncing out to a rain-shrouded reef to see the sort of darting fish I could view in comfort at any public aquarium, or indeed dental waiting room, was not enticing. According to the morning paper, a 2.3-metre swell was expected. I asked Allan, who once owned a sailing boat and a captain's cap and thus fancies himself an accomplished mariner, how big this was and he lifted his eyebrows in the manner of one impressed. 'Oh, that's big,' he said. This led him to tell me many happy anecdotes of being pitched about in terrifying seas, some of them involving boats not tied to a dock. As we sat there, one of the members of the staff breezed past.

'Cyclone coming!' she said perkily.

'Today?' I asked in what was becoming a customary bleat.

'Maybe!'

Our reef tour included pick-up at our hotel and transfer by coach to the boat at Port Douglas, twenty miles up the coast. The bus drew up at eight fifty, on time to the minute. As we climbed aboard, the driver was giving a rundown on marine stingers, with vivid descriptions of people who had failed to their cost to heed the warning signs. He assured us, however, there were no jellyfish on the reef. Unaccountably, he failed to mention reef sharks, boxfish, scorpionfish, stinging corals, sea snakes or the infamous grouper, a 900-pound monster that occasionally, through a combination of testiness and stupidity, chomps off a swimmer's arm or leg, then remembers that it doesn't like the taste of human flesh and spits it out.

I can't tell you how pleased I was when we arrived at Port Douglas to find that the boat was huge – as big as an English Channel ferry or very nearly – and sleekly new. I was also pleased, for their sake and mine, that none of the crew seemed to be manifesting any of the more obvious signs of dengue fever.[1] As we lined up with other arriving coach passengers I learned from a crew member that the ship held 450 and that 310 people were booked today. He also told me that the trip to the reef took ninety minutes and that the seas should be relatively benign. It was thirty-eight nautical miles to Agincourt Reef, where we would moor. This was, I noted with more than passing interest, the place where [an] American couple had gone missing.

When we got aboard they announced the free distribution of seasickness tablets to anyone who wanted. I was the first to the table.

'This is awfully thoughtful of you,' I said as I swilled down a handful.

'Well, it's better'n having people spewing up all over the shop,' said the girl brightly, and it was hard to argue with that.

The trip to the reef was smooth, as promised. What's more the sun came out, albeit weakly, turning the water from a leaden grey to an approximation of cobalt. While Allan went off to the sun deck to see if there were any women with large breasts to look at, I settled down with my notes.

Depending on which sources you consult, the Great Barrier Reef covers 280,000 square kilometres or 344,000 or something in between; stretches 1200 miles from top to bottom, or 1600; is bigger than Kansas or Italy or the United Kingdom. Nobody can agree really on where the Barrier Reef begins and ends, though everyone agrees it's awfully big. Even by the shortest measure, it is equivalent to the west coast of the

---

[1] ***dengue fever:*** a viral disease transmitted by mosquitoes

United States. And it is of course an immensely vital habitat – the oceanic equivalent of the Amazon rainforest. The Great Barrier Reef contains at least 1500 species of fish, 400 types of coral and 4000 varieties of molluscs, but those are essentially just guesses. No one has ever attempted a comprehensive survey. Too big a job.

Because it consists of some 3000 separate reefs and over 600 islands some people insist that it is not a single entity and therefore cannot accurately be termed the largest living thing on earth. That seems to me a little like saying that Los Angeles is not a city because it consists of lots of separate buildings. It hardly matters. It is fabulous. And it is all thanks to trillions of little coral polyps working with a dedicated and microscopic diligence over 18 million years, each adding a grain or two of thickness before expiring in a self-created silicate tomb. Hard not to be impressed.

As the ship began to make the sort of slowing-down noises that suggested imminent arrival, I went out on deck to join Allan. I had expected that we would be arriving at some kind of sandy atoll,[2] possibly with a beach bar and with a thatched roof, but in fact there was nothing but open sea all around, and a long ruff of gently breaking water, which I presumed indicated the sunken and unseen reef. In the middle of this scene sat an immense aluminium pontoon,[3] two storeys high and big enough to accommodate 400 day trippers. It brought to mind, if vaguely, an oil platform. This was to be our home for the next several hours. When the boat had docked, we all filed happily off. A loudspeaker outlined our many options. We could loll in the sun in deckchairs, or descend to an underwater viewing chamber, or grab snorkels and flippers for a swim, or board a semisubmersible ship for a tour of the reef in comfort.

We went first on the semisubmersible, a vessel in which thirty or forty people at a time could crowd into a viewing chamber below the waterline.

---

[2] **atoll:** circular coral reef surrounding a lagoon
[3] **pontoon:** a watertight float

Well, it was wonderful. No matter how much you read about the special nature of the Barrier Reef, nothing really prepares you for the sight of it. The pilot took us into a shimmery world of steep coral canyons and razor-edged defiles,[4] fabulously colourful and teeming with schools of fish of incredible variety and size – butterfly fish, damselfish, angelfish, parrotfish, the gorgeously colourful harlequin tuskfish, tubular pipefish. We saw giant clams and sea slugs and starfish, small forests of waving anemones and the pleasingly large and dopey potato cod. It was, as I had expected, precisely like being at a public aquarium, except of course that this was entirely wild and natural. I was amazed, no doubt foolishly, by what a difference this made. As I looked out a great turtle swam past, just a couple of yards from the window and quite indifferent to us. Then, furtively poking about on the bottom, was a reef shark – only a couple of feet long but capable of giving you a jolly good nip. It wasn't just the darting fish and other creatures, but the way the light filtered down from above, and the shape and texture and incredible variety of the coral itself. I was captivated beyond description.

Back on the pontoon, Allan insisted we go at once for a swim. At one side of the pontoon metal steps led into the water. At the top of the steps were large bins containing flippers, snorkels and masks. We kitted up and plopped in. I had assumed that we would be in a few feet of water, so I was taken aback – I am putting this mildly – to discover that I was perhaps sixty feet above the bottom. I had never been in water this deep before and it was unexpectedly unnerving – as unnerving as finding myself floating sixty feet in the air above solid ground. This panicky assessment took place over the course of perhaps three seconds, then my mask and snorkel filled with water and I started choking. Gasping peevishly, I dumped the water out and tried again, but almost immediately the mask filled again. I repeated the exercise two or three times more, but with the same result.

Allan, meanwhile, was shooting about like Darryl Hannah in *Splash.*

---

[4] **defiles:** narrow passes

'For God's sake, Bryson, what are you doing?' he said. 'You're three feet from the pontoon and you're drowning.'

'I am drowning.' I caught a roll of wave full in the face and came out of it sputtering. 'I'm a son of the soil,' I gasped. 'This is not my milieu.'

He clucked and disappeared. I dipped my head lightly under to see him shooting off like a torpedo in the direction of a colourful Maori wrasse – an angelfish the size of a sofa cushion – and was consumed once more with a bubbly dismay at all the clear, unimagined depth beneath me. There were big things down there, too – fish half as big as me and far more in their element than I was. Then my mask filled and I was sputtering again. Then another small rolling wave smacked me in the face. I must confess that I liked this even less – quite a good deal less – than I had expected to, and I hadn't expected to like it much.

Interestingly, I later learned that this is quite a common reaction among inexperienced ocean swimmers. They get in the water, discover that they are way out of their comfort zone, quietly panic and faint (a Japanese speciality, apparently) or have a heart attack (a fat person speciality). Now here's where the second interesting aspect comes in. Because snorkellers lie on the water with their arms and legs spread and their faces just under the surface – that is, in the posture known as the dead man's float – it isn't actually possible (or so I am told) to tell which people are snorkelling and which are dead. It's only when the whistle blows and everyone gets out except for one oddly inert and devoted soul that they know there will be one less for tea.

Fortunately, as you will have deduced from the existence of this book, I escaped this unhappy fate and managed to haul myself back onto the pontoon. I took a seat on a deckchair in the mild sunshine and towelled off with Allan's shirt.

A *See pages 120–122 for related activities.*

Mrs Puri's Plumbing

Water is often in short supply in India as William Dalrymple discovers almost as soon as he arrives in Delhi. This passage tells of economies considered necessary and of the importance of keeping up appearances.

William Dalrymple
from *City of Djinns* (1994)

The flat perched at the top of the house, little more than a lean-to riveted to Mrs Puri's ceiling. The stairwell exuded sticky, airless September heat; the roof was as thin as corrugated iron.

Inside we were greeted by a scene from *Great Expectations*; a thick pall of dust on every surface, a family of sparrows nesting in the blinds and a fleece of old cobwebs – great arbours of spider silk – arching the corner walls. Mrs Puri stood at the doorway, a small, bent figure in a *salwar kameez.*[1]

'The last tenant did not go out much,' she said, prodding the cobwebs with her walking stick. She added: 'He was not a tidy gentleman.' Olivia blew on a cupboard; the dust was so thick you could sign your name in it.

Our landlady, though a grandmother, soon proved herself to be a formidable woman. A Sikh from Lahore, Mrs Puri was expelled from her old home during Partition and in the upheavals of 1947 lost everything. She arrived in Delhi on a bullock cart. Forty-two years later she had made the transition from refugee pauper to Punjabi princess. She was now very rich indeed. She owned houses all over Delhi and had swapped her bullock for a fleet of new Maruti cars, the much coveted replacement for the old Hindustan Ambassador. Mrs Puri also controlled a variety of business interests. These included the Gloriana Finishing School, India's first etiquette college, a unique institution which taught village girls how

---

[1] ***salwar kameez:*** Indian dress

to use knives and forks, apply lipstick and make polite conversation about the weather.

Mrs Puri had achieved all this through a combination of hard work and good old-fashioned thrift. In the heat of the summer she rarely put on the air conditioning. In winter she allowed herself the electric fire for only half an hour a day. She recycled newspapers we threw out; and returning from parties late at night we could see her still sitting up, silhouetted against the window, knitting sweaters for export. 'Sleep is silver,' she would say in explanation, 'but money is gold.'

This was all very admirable, but the hitch, we soon learned, was that she expected tenants to emulate the disciplines she imposed upon herself. One morning, after only a week in the flat, I turned on the tap to discover that our water had been cut off, so went downstairs to sort out the problem. Mrs Puri had already been up and about for several hours; she had been to the gurdwara,[2] said her prayers and was now busy drinking her morning glass of rice water.

'There is no water in our flat this morning, Mrs Puri.'

'No, Mr William, and I am telling you why.'

'Why, Mrs Puri?'

'You are having guests, Mr William. And always they are going to the lavatory.'

'But why should that affect the water supply?'

'Last night I counted seven flushes,' said Mrs Puri, rapping her stick on the floor. 'So I have cut off the water as protest.'

She paused to let the enormity of our crime sink in.

'Is there any wonder that there is water shortage in our India when you people are making seven flushes in one night?'

Old Mr Puri, her husband, was a magnificent-looking Sikh gentleman with a long white beard and a tin zimmer frame with wheels on the

---

[2] **gurdwara:** Sikh place of worship

bottom. He always seemed friendly enough – as we passed he would nod politely from his armchair. But when we first took the flat Mrs Puri drew us aside and warned us that her husband had never been, well, quite the same since the riots that followed Mrs Gandhi's death in 1984.

It was a rather heroic story. When some hooligans began to break down the front door, Mr Puri got Ladoo (the name means Sweety), his bearer, to place him directly behind the splintering wood. Uttering a blood-curdling cry, he whipped out his old service revolver and fired the entire magazine through the door. The marauders ran off to attack the taxi rank around the corner and the Puris were saved.

From that day on, however, the old man had become a fervent Sikh nationalist. 'Everyone should have their own home,' he would snort. 'The Muslims have Pakistan. The Hindus have Hindustan. The Punjab is our home. If I was a young man I would join Bhindranwale and fight these Hindu dogs.'

'It is only talk,' Mrs Puri would reply.

'Before I die I will see a free Khalistan.'

'You are daydreaming only. How many years are left?'

'The Punjab is my home.'

'He may have been born in the Punjab,' Mrs Puri would say, turning to me, 'but now he could not go back to village life. He likes flush toilet and Star TV. Everybody likes flush toilet and Star TV. How can you leave these things once you have tasted such luxury?'

Since the riots, Mr Puri had also become intermittently senile. One day he could be perfectly lucid; the next he might suffer from the strangest hallucinations. On these occasions conversations with him took on a somewhat surreal quality:

MR PURI (up the stairs to my flat) Mr William! Get your bloody mules out of my room this minute!

WD But Mr Puri, I don't have any mules.

MR PURI Nonsense! How else could you get your trunks up the stairs?

During our first month in the flat, however, Mr Puri was on his best behaviour. Apart from twice proposing marriage to my wife, he behaved with perfect decorum.

It had been a bad monsoon. Normally in Delhi, September is a month of almost equatorial fertility and the land seems refreshed and newly-washed. But in the year of our arrival, after a parching summer, the rains had lasted for only three weeks. As a result dust was everywhere and the city's trees and flowers all looked as if they had been lightly sprinkled with talcum powder.

Nevertheless the air was still sticky with damp-heat, and it was in a cloud of perspiration that we began to unpack and to take in the eccentricities of our flat: the chiming doorbell that played both the Indian national anthem and 'Land of Hope and Glory'; the geyser, which if left on too long, would shoot a fountain of boiling water from an outlet on the roof and bathe the terrace in a scalding shower; the pretty round building just below the garden which we first took to be a temple, and only later discovered to be the local sewage works.

But perhaps the strangest novelty of coming to live in India – stranger even than Mrs Puri – was getting used to life with a sudden glut of domestic help. Before coming out to Delhi we had lived impecuniously[3] in a tiny student dive in Oxford. Now we had to make the transition to a life where we still had only two rooms, but suddenly found ourselves with more than twice that number of servants. It wasn't that we particularly wanted or needed servants; but, as Mrs Puri soon made quite clear, employing staff was a painful necessity on which the prestige of her household depended.

The night we moved in, we spent our first hours dusting and cleaning before sinking, exhausted, into bed at around 2 am. The

---

[3] **impecuniously:** without money

following morning we were woken at 7.30 sharp by 'Land of Hope and Glory'. Half asleep, I shuffled to the door to find Ladoo, Mr Puri's bearer, waiting outside. He was holding a tray. On the tray were two glasses of milky Indian *chai.*

'*Chota hazari*, sahib,' said Ladoo. Bed tea.

'What a nice gesture,' I said returning to Olivia. 'Mrs Puri has sent us up some tea.'

'I wish she had sent it up two hours later,' said Olivia from beneath her sheets.

I finished the tea and sank down beneath the covers. Ten seconds later the Indian national anthem chimed out. I scrambled out of bed and again opened the door. Outside was a thin man with purple, betel-stained[4] lips. He had a muffler wrapped around his head and, despite the heat, a thick donkey-jacket was buttoned tightly over his torso. I had never seen him before.

'*Mali*,' he said. The gardener.

He bowed, walked past me and made for the kitchen. From the bedroom I could hear him fiddling around, filling a bucket with water then splashing it over the plants on the roof terrace. He knocked discreetly on the bedroom door to indicate he had finished, then disappeared down the stairs. The *mali* was followed first by Murti, the sweeper, then by Prasad, the *dhobi*, and finally by Bahadur, Mrs Puri's Nepali cook. I gave up trying to sleep and went downstairs.

'Mrs Puri,' I said. 'There has been a stream of strange people pouring in and out of my flat since seven-thirty.'

'I know, Mr William,' replied Mrs Puri. 'These people are your servants.'

'But I don't want any servants.'

'Everyone has servants,' said Mrs Puri. 'You must have servants too. This is what these people are for.'

---

[4] ***betel-stained:*** stained by the seed and leaves of a palm

I frowned. 'But must we have so many?'

'Well, you must have a cook and a bearer.'

'We don't need a bearer. And both of us enjoy cooking.'

'In that case you could have one cook-bearer. One man, two jobs. Very modern. Then there is the *mali*, the sweeper, and a *dhobi* for your washing. Also you must be having one driver.' Mrs Puri furrowed her brow. 'It is very important to have good chauffeur,' she said gravely. 'Some pukka fellow with a smart uniform.'

'I haven't got a car. So it's pointless having a driver.'

'But if you have no car and no driver,' said Mrs Puri, 'how will you be getting from place to place?'

See pages 120–122 for related activities.

The Takla Makan Desert

The Swedish geographer and explorer, Sven Hedin (1869–1952), was a very experienced traveller who had known Siberian winters, burning deserts and the highest of mountain peaks. He wrote a diary as he journeyed across the Takla Makan Desert in 1894 and it was published in 1926 in My Life as an Explorer. Takla Makan *means 'he who enters will never leave' and, as this extract from Hedin's diary shows, this seemed almost to predict that his crossing of the great desert could well have been his final journey.*

Sven Hedin

from *My Life as an Explorer* (1926)

May 1st. The night was cold; the thermometer fell to 35° Fahr. (2°C.), the lowest reading we had during the twenty-six days we were crossing the desert. But the atmosphere was pure, and the stars glittered with incomparable brilliancy. The morning dawned calm and gloriously bright – not a speck of cloud in the sky, not a breath of wind on the tops of the dunes. No sooner had the sun risen than it began to be warm ... All the previous day I had not tasted a drop of water. But suffering the extreme tortures of thirst, I ventured to swallow about a tumblerful of the horrible and abominable concoction which the Chinese call brandy, stuff that we carried to burn in our Primus cooking-stove. It burned my throat like oil of vitriol ... In the still atmosphere the funereal camels' bells rang out clearer than ever before. We had left three graves behind us. How many more were we destined to leave by the side of our track? The funeral procession was rapidly approaching the churchyard.

Was there *no* means of imparting moisture to our bodies before we left this hateful spot – even though it were only a moistening of the lips and throat? We were all suffering incredible agonies of thirst, the men more than I. My eyes chanced to fall upon the cock that still remained alive. He was walking about amongst the camels with all the gravity of his kind. Why not tap and drink his blood? One of the men made an incision in the animal's neck. The blood trickled out slowly, and in small quantity. It was not enough; we wanted more. Yet another innocent life must be sacrificed. But the men hesitated a long time before they could bring themselves to slaughter our docile travelling-companion, the sheep, which had followed us through every danger with the fidelity of a dog. But I told them, it was to save our own lives, which might be prolonged a little if we drank the sheep's blood.

May 4th. Kasim [the only other man still alive] was sinking fast. He was incapable of digging a hole in the sand to lie in; and, as he was also unable to cover me with cool sand, I suffered terribly from the heat. All day long we never spoke a word. Indeed, what was there we could talk about? Our thoughts were the same, our apprehensions the same. The fact is we really could not talk; we could only whisper or hiss out our words.

May 5th. Still we toiled on for life – bare life. Then imagine our surprise, our amazement, when on the long sloping surface of a dune we perceived human footsteps imprinted in the sand!

We followed up the trail till we came to the top of a dune, where the sand was driven together in a hard compact mass, and the footprints could be more distinctly made out.

Kasim dropped on his knees; then cried in a scarcely audible voice, 'They are our own footsteps!'

May 7th. Shortly before five o'clock we came to a *darah* (strictly speaking, valley) or depression in the sand, and I soon arrived at the conclusion, that it was a former bed of the river. Numerous poplars grew in its lowest part. There must be water nor very far below them. Once more we seized the spade; but we had not strength enough to dig. We were forced to struggle on again towards the east.

We travelled at first across a belt of low, barren sand. But at half-past five we entered a thick, continuous forest.

I called upon Kasim to come with me to the water. But he was beaten at last. He shook his head, and with a gesture of despair, signed to me to go on alone, drink, and bring back water to him. Otherwise he would just die where he lay.

I now changed my course to due south-east. Why so? Why did I not keep on towards the east, as I had always done hitherto? I do not know. Perhaps the moon bewitched me; for she showed her silver crescent in that quarter of the heavens and shed down a dim, pale blue illumination over the silent scene. Leaning on the spade-shaft, I plodded away at a steady pace in a straight line towards the south-east, as though I were being led by an unseen, but irresistible, hand. At intervals I was seized by a traitorous desire to sleep, and was obliged to stop and rest. My pulse was excessively weak; I could scarcely discern its beats. I had to steel myself by the strongest effort of will to prevent myself from dropping off to sleep. I was afraid that if I did go off, I should never waken again. I walked with my eyes riveted upon the moon, and kept expecting to see its silver belt glittering on the dark waters of the stream. But no such sight met my eyes. The whole of the east quarter was enshrouded in the cold night mist.

After going about a mile and a half, I was at length able to distinguish the dark line of the forest on the right bank of the river. It gradually became more distinct as I advanced. There was a thicket of bushes and reeds; a poplar blown down by the wind lay across a deep hole in the river-bed. I was only a few yards from the bank when a wild-duck, alarmed by my approach, flew up and away as swift as an arrow. I heard a splash, and in the next moment I stood on the brink of a little pool filled with fresh, cool water – beautiful water!

It would be vain for me to try to describe the feelings which now overpowered me. They may be imagined; they cannot be described.

See pages 120–122 for related activities.

The Aswan Dam

In the 1990s Stanley Stewart set out to visit the source of the River Nile,
travelling the length of Egypt, through the Sudan and on to Uganda. The
river was a constant companion – always at the heart of the journey. In
this extract he describes the artificial lake at Aswan, the result of the
building of a dam and the flooding of huge areas of land that took the
homes of 50 000 people.

Stanley Stewart
from *Old Serpent Nile* (1991)

Old Wadi Halfa had been a delightful riverside town full of palm trees and fine houses. It had a population of 11 000 people. It lies now beneath the water of the lake, about ten miles out from the shore. Its inhabitants, with the inhabitants of all drowned villages of Sudanese Nubia, were transported to Khashm el-Girba, east of Khartoum, almost 600 miles away.

A few people remained to take up lives in the new Wadi Halfa, a bleak tenuous place which sprang up where the railway line from Khartoum comes to an apparently arbitrary end against a low wall of sleepers. There are no streets and no trees. The plain-faced buildings sit in the desert like tents, straggling flocks of goats wander among them searching for scraps.

The bleakness of the place was exacerbated by the heat. From eleven in the morning until four in the afternoon nothing stirred. We were there in September when the daytime temperatures never fell below 100°F, and at midday were closer to 110°. We longed for the arrival of autumn, but began to doubt that such a season existed in Sudan. We were to wait another six weeks before the fierce summer heat showed any sign of breaking.

The buildings of Halfa all face north to avoid the worst of the sun and to catch the northerly breezes. In the souk[1] were dim shops which sold batteries and bottles of scent and boxes of safety pins. The teahouses were poor places with earthen floors and blackened walls, and the fruit and vegetable sellers, squatting beneath awnings, were all specialists who sold only one kind of produce each. They arranged them on the sand – lemons or onions or oranges – in careful little piles and sold them for so much a pile. The prices were fantastic, far higher than in Egypt. Sudan was a land of scarcity where fresh vegetables, and much else, were luxuries.

Of tailors, Halfa had no shortage. There seemed to be scores of them in the town. In the mornings they worked outside in the streets on their ancient pedal machines, raising a loud chorus of whirring. At midday they retreated into the cool darkness of their shops. They worked only in white, for unlike the Egyptians, Sudanese men wore only white gallibayas[2] and pantaloons. The women made up for this restraint. In the streets, over their house clothes, they wore splendid full-length wraps, called tōbs, of the most startling colours and patterns.

At one end of the town was a bank where we went on our first day to change some money. It was a big dusty room with a wide counter. The clerk looked at us uneasily, torn between his duty and his better instincts.

'Do not change money here,' he whispered. 'Go to the shops. They will give you a much better black-market rate.'

We stayed in a hotel near the railway station, a humble place of three adjoining courtyards. The hotel was blue. The floors of the rooms were covered with cracked blue and white tiles, the walls were a pale blue wash flaking on to the sand and the doors a bright sea blue. In the centre of each courtyard were large earthenware water jugs which sweated

---

[1] **souk:** open-air market
[2] **gallibayas:** long, flowing garments

gently in the breeze under the shade of thatched canopies. They were replenished each evening with barrels of muddy water brought from the lake on donkey carts.

We ventured out only in the mornings and the evenings when the sun was low and the shadows of the tall robed figures stretched to impossible lengths across the sands. The afternoons we passed in the hotel courtyard where we ate, read, played cards and slept like cats in a paradise of shade, northerly breezes and birdsong, while the town baked outside.

The terrific heat of northern Sudan is the inspiration for the peripatetic[3] bed. Life in a Sudanese hotel revolves around the courtyard and the bed, usually a light metal cot with a thin mattress. The room is of no consequence. It is unfurnished and used only to store your baggage.

During the day the bed is moved into the shade of the arcades around the courtyard where you sit or lie upon it outside your door, and catch whatever breeze is going. In the evening the beds move out from under the arcades into the courtyard itself where you spend the night sleeping under the stars with your fellow guests. In the morning the beds return to the gentle shade of the arcades.

What this arrangement lacks in privacy it gains in congeniality. Friendships quickly develop as guests help each other carry their beds back and forth.

We shared our courtyard with a large colony of sparrows, who resided in two stunted trees, and a company of merchants from Berber. The merchants were a cheerful but rather mysterious lot. In answer to our enquiries they said they were waiting for goods coming from Egypt to receive customs clearance. We thought we detected more than a hint of irony in this answer, and we suspected that they were smugglers. They dressed well and were seemingly unconcerned about their long wait in what was not Halfa's cheapest hotel. Like everyone else they spent their

---

[3] ***peripatetic:*** moveable

days lounging in the arcades of the courtyards. In the mornings we would see them in the souk holding hands with strange men.

The merchants were devout Muslims and their prayers in the patchy shade of the two courtyard trees, prefaced by elaborate washing, punctuated the day. They were dismissive, however, of President Numeri and his introduction of Sharia, Islamic law, which demanded the amputation of the hands of thieves and forbade all alcohol under threat of public flogging.

'You must not worry about these laws,' they said. 'They apply only in Khartoum. Here in Wadi Halfa, in Dongola, in Berber, everywhere else, these laws do not matter.'

In the evenings the merchants invited us to join them as they sat chatting on their cots in the middle of the courtyard. Gas lanterns at their feet threw deep shadows across their faces. The oldest reminded us of the barge captain. Next to him were two brothers, tall beautiful men with liquid eyes and graceful hands. Opposite them was a small elfin fellow who wore a shiny blue waistcoat over his gallibaya.

The merchants were handing round a five-litre plastic jug of the kind normally used to carry petrol. Each drank from it in turn. They handed it to us, and waited for our response. It was *seiko*, a clear spirit made from dates which tasted rather like home-made grappa without the subtlety.

I blew through my lips as if I was breathing fire.

'Very good,' I said.

They laughed and clapped me on the back and handed the container round the circle again.

'If you throw it up in the air,' the elfin one said, 'it will evaporate before it reaches the ground. But we will not try it. It is a sin to waste the gifts of Allah.'

Later the men began to sing for us, sitting forward on the edge of their cots. The songs were slow and melodic. They sang very softly, at times almost whispering the words. The songs were about love and loss, aspiration and disappointment, but the men smiled as they sang, as if the melodies and the sheer pleasure of singing overcame the tragedy of the words.

Wadi Halfa was a town of transients,[4] waiting on the boat to Egypt or the train to Khartoum. Both appeared about twice a week. They were meant to coincide so that travellers would have a smooth connection, but they rarely did, and the tea-houses and cheap hotels of Halfa were swollen with travellers who invariably had to wait for days.

We became regulars at a tea stall in the open desert between our hotel and the souk which served delicious spiced and milky Sudanese tea. There were no tables and one sat on the sand to eat. At night the stall was lit with gas lanterns and the sands beyond their uncertain light were crowded with shadowy figures eating and drinking. In spite of the sacrifice it had made for the High Dam at Aswan, whose turbines generated megawatts of electrical power, Wadi Halfa still had no electricity.

The owner of the stall reminisced about old Wadi Halfa where his father had owned a big tea-house on the Corniche. It had been a most beautiful place, he said, before the flood. 'There were fine buildings all along the river, a long avenue of palm trees, perfectly straight, beautiful mosques and many beautiful houses. Not like here.' He gestured towards the darkness beyond the circle of light. 'You could have stayed in the Nile Hotel. All the rooms looked over the gardens which ran right down to the river. The flood took everything. The last part of old Halfa to disappear was the minaret of the Tawfikia mosque.'

Fifty thousand Sudanese lost their homes to the rising waters of Lake Nasser. Twenty-seven villages, as well as the town of Wadi Halfa, were submerged. The administrator in charge of compensation and resettlement was Hassan Dafalla, an intelligent and sensitive man who managed a

---

[4] ***transients:*** travelling people

difficult task with considerable skill. He was one of the last people to leave the old town of Wadi Halfa after its inhabitants had been transported south, and he has left a chilling account of the empty town's last days.

The deluge began on the first day of September 1963. Dafalla woke to find the railway station yard covered with water, and half a mile of track submerged. In the early afternoon the river breached its bank opposite the Tawfikia mosque and invaded part of the market. Later in the afternoon the embankment at El Geiger was overwhelmed and water surrounded the Ismaili mosque.

The following day the entire market area was submerged, and the shops, built of mud-brick, melted like biscuits, leaving islands of rubble in a brown lake. The hospital was encircled and parts of it began to collapse. Water rushed across the road to the Nile Hotel, carrying scorpions and reptiles into the drowning rooms.

In the evening Dafalla found the waters were seeping into the gardens of his own house. Shrubs, which had been dying from lack of water since the supply had been cut off, were suddenly green and straight again in a brief moment of health before the rising waters overwhelmed them. Rats living in the storerooms of his house emerged from their holes, carrying their young in their teeth, and ran to higher ground.

That night, worried about the water entering his house as he slept, he left the edge of his bedsheet dangling on the ground so that the water would awaken him. In the morning he found the Nile had reached his garden parapet. Soon only the grove of palm trees, the waters rising up their trunks, showed where the houses had stood.

I was reminded of Isidora whose mummy we had seen at Tuna el-Gebel and of a recurring paradox, destruction by the forces of creation. The further we went up the Nile, the more the river seemed to express some awful ambivalence.

A *See pages 120–122 for related activities.*

Homecomings

Journeys are wonderful things, they leave you with the memories of people, places and experiences that are part of you forever. The setting out is always a moment of excitement, of hopes and dreams and some times a touch of nervousness. The homecoming is a time of mixed feelings too – delight at the prospect of seeing friends and family, a sense of achievement at a planned journey completed and often a desperate need for the food of home denied you for so long!

Here are just three homecomings.

Finis

In One's Company *Peter Fleming tells the story of a seven-month journey through China in 1933. He calls his book 'a superficial account of an unsensational journey' – it seems very different to the reader as it offers a glimpse into the world untravelled by foreigners. He was often in danger and needed great energy and endurance and, in these final pages of his book, he considers the advantages of lone travel.*

Peter Fleming
from *One's Company* (1934)

Lights pricked the dust between wind and water. I stood on deck and watched England swim towards us, a long indeterminate ribbon of opacity which widened slowly. Around me my fellow-passengers were preparing for the supreme moment, the moment of homecoming ...

'Oh, *there* you are. I thought you were never coming ... '

'What did you do with my landing card?'

'But you said *you* were going to tip the wine-steward ... '

'Well you'll just have to unpack the book and give it back to her.'

'How should *I* know?'

'You can't have looked properly, that's all I can say ... '

'Yes, dear, I know, but ... '

'There's not time, I tell you.'

'No, sir, I haven't seen her.'

'You *don't* mean to say you've lost the keys?'

'She says she won't come up till the ship docks.'

'You might have known we'd want some change ... '

'Oh, well, have it your own way.'

'If you don't declare them, I shall.'

'George is quite old enough to look after his own things.'

'It's not *my* fault ... '

'Hi! Maude! *Maude* ... '

Travelling by one's self, I reflected has many advantages. Katherine Mansfield once wrote in her *Journal*, 'Even if I should, by some awful chance, find a hair upon my bread and honey – at any rate it is my own hair'. There are moments in every journey when the equanimity of even the most fatalistic traveller breaks down and he stands revealed in an unbecoming posture of dejection, panic, or annoyance. If he is alone, the moment passes, damaging only his self-respect; if he is not alone, its effects are less ephemeral. Somebody else's bread and honey has been spoilt.

It is easy enough for one man to adapt himself to living under strange and constantly changing conditions. It is much harder for two. Leave A or B alone in a distant country, and each will evolve a congenial *modus vivendi*. Throw them together, and the comforts of companionship are as likely as not offset by the strain of reconciling their divergent methods. A likes to start early and halt for a siesta; B does not feel the heat and insists on sleeping late. A instinctively complies with regulations. B instinctively defies them. A finds it impossible to pass a temple, B finds it impossible to pass a bar. A is cautious, B is rash. A is indefatigable, B tires easily. A needs a lot of food, B very little. A snores, B smokes a pipe in bed ...

Each would get on splendidly by himself. Alone together, they build up gradually between them a kind of unacknowledged rivalry. Allowances are always being made, precedents established; each, in his darker moments, looks back on the journey they are making and sees it lined, as if by milestones, with little monuments to his own self-sacrificing tolerance. Each, while submitting readily to the exotic customs of the country, endures with a very bad grace the trifling idiosyncrasies of the other. The complex structure of their relationship, with its queer blend of nobility and baseness, its accretion of unforeseen drawbacks and unforeseen compensations, bulks larger and larger, obtruding itself between them and the country they are visiting, blotting it out ...

Occasionally you find the ideal companion; exactly a year ago I had returned to England with such a one. But the ideal companion is rare, and in default of him it is better to make a long journey alone. One's company in a strange world.

See pages 123–124 for related activities.

Kathmandu and Home to Delhi

As a student, the now famous novelist Vikram Seth hitchhiked from his Chinese university. He travelled through China, all the way across Tibet, on to Nepal and home to Delhi. The extract here sees him in Kathmandu almost at his journey's end.

Vikram Seth
from *From Heaven Lake* (1983)

I get a cheap room in the centre of town and sleep for hours. The next morning, with Mr Shah's son and nephew, I visit the two temples in Kathmandu that are most sacred to Hindus and Buddhists.

At Pashupatinath (outside which a sign proclaims 'Entrance for the Hindus only') there is an atmosphere of febrile confusion. Priests, hawkers, devotees, tourists, cows, monkeys, pigeons and dogs roam through the grounds. We offer a few flowers. There are so many worshippers that some people trying to get the priest's attention are elbowed aside by others pushing their way to the front. A princess of the Nepalese royal house appears; everyone bows and makes way. By the main gate, a party of saffron-clad Westerners struggle for permission to enter. The policeman is not convinced that they are 'the Hindus'. A fight breaks out between two monkeys. One chases the other, who jumps onto a *shivalingà*, then runs screaming around the temples and down to the river, the holy Bagmati, that flows below. A corpse is being cremated on its banks; washerwomen are at their work and children bathe. From a balcony a basket of flowers and leaves, old offerings now wilted, is dropped into the river. A stone image of a Nandi bull sits firmly between two competing *sadhus*, each muttering his mantra, each keeping a careful but hopeful eye on the passers-by. A small shrine half protrudes from the stone platform on the river bank.

When it emerges fully, the goddess inside will escape, and the veil period of the Kaliyug will end on earth.

At the Baudhnath stupa,[1] the Buddhist shrine of Kathmandu, there is, in contrast, a sense of stillness. Its immense white dome is ringed by a road. Small shops stand on its outer edge: many of these are owned by Tibetan immigrants; felt bags, Tibetan prints and silver jewellery can be bought here. There are no crowds: this is a haven of quietness in the busy streets around.

In Kathmandu I wind down after my journey. I luxuriate in my tiredness; drift deliciously along, all energy spent, allowing sight to follow sight, thought to follow thought, for now (apart from the easily fulfillable intention of returning to Delhi) there is nothing, no intermediate step that I must perform: there is no lift to look for, no hill to climb, no land to carry, no town en route. There are no papers that I have to obtain. For a person of fundamentally sedentary habits I have been wandering far too long; a continuously wandering life like Sui's would drive me crazy. I marvel at those travellers who, out of curiosity or a sense of mission, wander through unfamiliar environments for years on end. It requires an attitude of mind more capable of contentment with the present than my own. My drive to arrive is too strong. At many points in this journey, impatience has displaced enjoyment. This tension is the true cause of my exhaustion. When I am back in Delhi I will not move for a month, just sit at home, talk with my family and friends, read, rewind, sleep.

Kathmandu is vivid, mercenary, religious, with small shrines to flower-adorned deities along the narrowest and busiest streets; with fruitsellers, flutesellers, hawkers of postcards and pornography; shops selling Western cosmetics, film rolls and chocolate; or copper utensils and Nepalese antiques. Film songs blare out from the radios, car horns sound, bicycle bells ring, stray cows low questioningly at motorcycles, vendors shout out their wares. I indulge myself mindlessly; buy a bar of Tobler marzipan, a

---

[1] ***stupa:*** domed building

corn-on-the-cob roasted in a charcoal brazier on the pavement (rubbed with salt, chilli powder and lemon); a couple of love story comics, and even a *Reader's Digest.* All this I wash down with Coca Cola and a nauseating orange drink, and feel much the better for it.

I discover that Indian currency is accepted on the Kathmandu streets at an exchange rate of 1.45 Nepalese rupees per Indian rupee. The Chinese exchange rates at the bank in Zhangmu were 0.149 yuan per Nepalese rupee and 0.162 yuan per Indian rupee. It occurs to me that the disparity in cross-rates could enable any habitual border-hopper to realise a tidy profit.

Using Indian currency to pay for a map of Nepal makes me feel quite dislocated. I consider what route I should take back home. If I were propelled by enthusiasm for travel *per se*, I would go by bus and train to Patna, then sail up the Ganges past Benares to Allahabad, then up the Jumna, past Agra to Delhi. But I am too exhausted and homesick; today is the last day of August. Go home, I tell myself: move directly towards home. I enter a Nepal Airlines office and buy a ticket for tomorrow's flight.

I look at the fluteseller standing in a corner of the square near the hotel. In his hand is a pole with an attachment at the top from which fifty or sixty *bansuris* protrude in all directions, like the quills of a porcupine. They are of bamboo: there are cross-flutes and recorders. From time to time he stands the pole on the ground, selects a flute and plays for a few minutes. The sound rises clearly above the noise of the traffic and the hawkers' cries. He plays slowly, meditatively, without excessive display. He does not shout out his wares. Occasionally he makes a sale, but in a curiously offhanded way as if this were incidental to his enterprise. Sometimes he breaks off playing to talk to the fruitseller. I imagine that this has been the pattern of his life for years.

I find it difficult to tear myself away from the square. Flute music always does this to me: it is at once the most universal and most particular of sounds. There is no culture that does not have its flute – the reed *neh,* the recorder, the Japanese *shakuhachi*, the deep *bansuri* of Hindustani classical music, the clear or breathy flutes of South America, the high-pitched Chinese flutes. Each has its specific fingering and compass. It weaves its own associations. Yet to hear any flute is, it seems to me, to be drawn into the commonalty of all mankind, to be moved by music closest in its phrases and sentences to the human voice. Its motive force too is living breath: it too needs to pause and breathe before it can go on.

That I can be so affected by a few familiar phrases on the *bansuri*, or by a piece of indigo paper surprises me at first, for on the previous occasions that I have returned home after a long absence abroad, I have hardly noticed such details, and certainly have not invested them with the significance I now do. I think it is the gradualness of my journey that has caused this. With air travel the shock of arrival is more immediate: the family, the country, the climate all strike with simultaneous impact, so that the mind is bewildered, and the particular implications of small things obscured.

As the evening comes on I walk to the Maidan, the open grass-covered common in the centre of Kathmandu. Goatherds drive their goats between the football players and the goal. The last overs of a cricket match are interrupted by a group of elder citizens taking a stroll across the pitch. I walk back to the hotel.

At 3.30 at night I am woken by insects. At five I am woken by the cooing of pigeons outside my window. At six I am woken by my alarm clock. I take a taxi to the airport. The plane is delayed, but by eleven o'clock we are airborne. Below lie the green hills of Nepal; in an hour I will be home. It will be the first time that my parents, my brother, my sister and I have been together in seven years. The family does not know where I am: I later discover that the telegram from Lhasa never did get to Delhi.

As I sit in my seat sipping tomato juice and adjusting my watch to New Delhi time, the whole of the last two months takes on a dreamy quality. I can more easily see myself standing outside a police station at Turfan than travelling through Anduo or Shigatse. Even having been to Tibet, it still strikes me as 'somewhere I would like to travel to', a place I feel I still know next to nothing about; yet I cannot imagine, once I am no longer a student, that I will ever have the means to return.

Almost to reassure myself that this journey did take place, I recite an incantation of names: Turfan, Urumqi, Liuyuan, Dunhuang, Nanhu ... – the images regain substance – ... Germu, Naqu, Lhasa, Shigatse, Nilamu, Zhangmu, Lamasangu, Kathmandu. But alongside these names there are others – Quzha, Sui, Norbu – that mean even more to me. I recall Quzha's comment: 'I'm glad things have improved in our relations.' It is a curiously innocent remark in a world where foreign relations are determined by little other than realpolitik.[2]

If India and China were amicable towards each other, almost half the world would be at peace. Yet friendship rests on understanding; and the two countries, despite their contiguity,[3] have had almost no contact in the course of history. Few travellers have made the journey over the Himalayas, and not many more have made the voyage by sea; trade, while it has existed, has always been constrained by geography. In Tibet and South East Asia we find a fusion of the two cultures; but the heartlands of the two great culture zones have been almost untouched by each other. The only important exception to this is the spread of Buddhism.

Unfortunately I think that this will continue to be the case: neither strong economic interest nor the natural affinities of a common culture tie India and China together. The fact that they are both part of the same landmass means next to nothing. There is no such thing as an Asian ethos or mode of thinking.

The best that can be hoped for on a national level is a respectful patience on either side as in, for instance, trying to solve the border

---

[2] **realpolitik:** a ruthlessly realistic approach to leadership, rather than a moralistic one
[3] **their contiguity:** being neighbouring countries

problem. But on a personal level, to learn about another great culture is to enrich one's life, to understand one's own country better, to feel more at home in the world, and indirectly to add to that reservoir of individual goodwill that may, generations from now, temper the cynical use of national power.

We touch down in Delhi at noon. The customs officer looks dubiously at the rice sack I am carrying over my shoulder and at the bottle of Glenfiddich I hold in my hand.

'Anything to declare?' He looks at the bottle.

'No. I got this at the duty free shop in Kathmandu.'

'Please open that ... thing.'

I place the gunny bag on the counter, and take out the objects inside, one by one, like Santa Claus. He passes his hand gingerly over the stone with '*Om mani padme hum*' inscribed on it. He taps my soap-box thoughtfully.

'All right. You can go.'

I am home in half an hour.

🅐 *See pages 123–124 for related activities.*

Full Circle

And to finish what we started here are the final two days of Michael Palin's diary.

Michael Palin

from *Around the World in 80 Days* (1989)

Day 78   11 December

Forty-eight hours to go before the deadline. Fogg at this stage was literally burning his boat in an attempt to get the *Henrietta* to Liverpool. He'd already got rid of the cabins, the bunks and the poop-deck. 'The next day ... they burned the masts, the rafts and the spars ... Passepartout, hewing, cutting, sawing, did the work of ten men. It was a perfect fury of demolition.' At least he was on the move. I have the uneasy feeling of being marooned.

In grey, characterless weather much like that when, eleven weeks ago today, I first caught sight of the French coast at Boulogne, we are coming alongside the almost deserted container port of Le Havre. It's all rather anti-climatic. I remember the captain's concern to get his ship unloaded before the dockers had their Sunday lunch. Well, it's turned 10 o'clock and we're not even tied up yet. The Southampton ferry has sailed and all Passepartout and I can do is sit and wait. Remembering the dockers and their Sunday lunch gives us an idea, and as the trucks begin to roll past the gantry cranes and the unloading begins at a decent, if not manic pace, Passepartout and I leave the *Leda Maersk* and set off in search of a French Sunday Lunch.

We pass the smartest ship in Le Havre docks; a white-hulled multi-decked cruise liner, not from Monte Carlo or Bermuda, but from Russia. She's the only thing that is smart in what is essentially an industrial complex, and the French, cultivators of the comfortable lifestyle, builders of handsome cities and attractive villages, are quite unsentimental when it comes to industry, so there's not much attempt to conceal the grime as we walk up beside a railway track with silos and warehouses on one side and the sad and derelict remains of the transatlantic passenger terminal on the other. That the glamour of the place where the great liners docked should be thus reduced is quite a shock and reminds me how long ago it was that I fell in love with Jane Russell in *The French Line*.

An hour's walk brings us at last into the town itself. The centre, destroyed by bombs in the Second World War, has been rebuilt without flair. Long low terraces are dull in scale and finish and present a dour background to the waterfront area. Quick look in the cathedral, from which people in their Sunday best are emerging after mass. A slightly mad-looking man is trying to get the priest's attention. The priest eventually throws him out.

In these unpromising surroundings we come across a restaurant which serves us a superb five-course lunch and which is by extraordinary and suitable coincidence designed like a railway train. It is family run and cramped in the French style, and we wonder if it's to save space that the patron employs his tiny son as a waiter. Nigel asks the boy his age. He looks about eleven but turns out to be even younger.

'He's seven,' translates Nigel after a brief conversation.

'No ... no!' the boy protests vigorously. 'Seventeen!'

We don't stint the wine, and drinking the likes of Sancerre and Gigondas after all we've been through is like finding a waterfall in the desert. The walk back to the *Leda Maersk* seems much shorter and more convivial, and though none of us is admitting it, this unscheduled lunch in Le Havre had a definite celebratory air.

We leave France at seven in the evening. The weather is settled. The Channel is millpond calm. There's a chill in the air as we move slowly out toward the harbour wall of the fishing port which Francis I christened Le Havre de Grace in 1516. Past the euphoniously named Bassin Théophile

Du Crocq and a last illuminated Christmas tree and onto the high seas again.

As soon as we're clear of the sodium glare of the city lights another wonderful night sky is revealed. It reminds me of nights on the Bay of Bengal, but as Captain Rodebaek points out, it's better. There's more to see in the northern sky.

The day ends with a party, of which I dimly remember a tug of war in which a BBC team, sapped by over-confidence and French Sunday lunch, were pulled to defeat, and a 16-person doubles table tennis tournament in which the Professor and myself triumphed by a whisker over Jesper and Erik the accountant.

At one point we listened to our recording of *Under Milk Wood*. Noel, the radio operator was so taken with it he asked for a copy to take back to his wife. Listening to it with him was particularly appropriate, for Noel has maintained the Indian presence that has been such a feature of my journey. If I were superstitious I'd say that this presence has brought us luck, and as I stand with a buzzing head at the deck rail at two in the morning, watching us turn North through the Straits of Dover on seas of almost freakish tranquillity, I think back to the twenty-eighth day when Jagjit Uppal told my fortune and wonder whether this whole journey wasn't made in Bombay. A last few deep breaths of sea air and back to my cabin to pack my bag and deflate my world for the last time.

Day 79   12 December

Four hours' sleep and up to catch the dawn over the Suffolk coast. A golden sun is rising slowly into a clear sky as we approach the low-lying, neat green shoreline, with Harwich's old church and surrounding houses sitting on their low headland and Felixstowe opposite. I didn't expect such a caricature of England. Felixstowe seems tiny compared to the ports I've visited round the world – a container terminal John Betjeman might have approved of. Not hugely out of scale with the undemonstrative coastline and giving way quite quickly to green fields beyond. There is hardly a ripple enough on the surface of the North Sea to ring the mournful bell on the big green buoy that stands at the entrance to the port. We are home on a morning of glassy calm.

The pilot is already on the bridge, supervising our approach. On this journey pilots have been like heralds, embodying the first sight and sounds of new places.

So I know exactly where I am as I hear, 'We're going to swing her in, we'll need two tugs,' spoken in the dry matter-of-fact English professional monotone. I'm back in police stations and Crown courts and customs sheds and airline cockpits and doctors' waiting rooms. 'Dead Slow,' he orders, and jokes to Captain Rodebaek about a friend who's just come back from a holiday in Spain: 'He got a whole year's rain in three days!'

The captain smiles but only out of habit. Maybe there is always this feeling of strain between captains and pilots.

With the tug *Brightwell* at our stern and *Victoria* of Liverpool at the bow, we wend our way between the marker buoys into the mouth of the Orwell. A seaman (and I realise that, unlike the *Garnet*, I know hardly any of the names of this crew) selects a Union Jack from the wooden pigeon holes full of national flags and goes outside to run it up the mast. The pilot talks to one of the tugs:

'Given her a helping hand, Victoria, starboard bow.'

We are aiming for a mooring beside *Canadian Explorer* of Hong Kong, and a Russian ship. Bente stands in the bow with her walkie-talkie, Danish flag fluttering above her, and blonde hair streaming from beneath her 'Maersk Line' baseball cap. A strange wild Nordic figure in her light blue deck overalls.

For me this is the end of an epic and unusual journey, I'm almost home. For Captain Rodebaek and his crew it's the first of a gruelling series of North Sea stop-overs. From Felixstowe they must cross to

Antwerp, from Antwerp to Bremerhaven and Bremerhaven to Hamburg, before turning and heading down the Channel again to Singapore. This is where the crews earn their money, and while TV presenters drool at sunrises, they have only a week of sleepless nights to look forward to.

I unfold a small piece of paper given to me by the jolly German chef as I said goodbye to him in the galley this morning. He said it summed up the sailor's lot, 'We the Willing, led by the Unknowing, are doing the impossible for the ungrateful. We have done so much for so long with so little, we are now qualified to do anything with nothing.' As we disembark, Passepartout admits to having supplemented the Professor's whisky bottle each night of the journey – four before he even noticed.

Have to keep reminding myself that it's not over yet, and will not be until I'm inside the Reform Club again. A *Leda Maersk* truck gives me a lift through the tidy, well-kept streets of Felixstowe, to the railway station. There is no train for an hour, so we repair to the Moat House Hotel across the road. Ironically the hotel bar has a colonial feel. The only other customers apart from ourselves are elderly ladies ordering scotch and sodas. I fantasise that they are the widows of men who travelled, maintaining the tradition of the quick snifter[1] before tiffin.[2] A young barmaid with strident lipstick plays listlessly with a beermat. Though I've been hurtling round the world, against the clock, my progress has been marked by moments like these, still pools at the side of a stream, where for a while, nothing at all moves.

At half-past twelve, well into my last twenty-four hours, I pick up the local two-car diesel and we rumble off towards Ipswich. England looks greener than anywhere else in the world. And much neater than I remember. On the Inter-City train from Ipswich to London I decide to treat myself to a Great British Lunch and receive instead a Great British Apology.

---

[1] **snifter:** small drink
[2] **tiffin:** a light midday meal

'I'm very sorry, sir, there's no chef and no food, but I can offer you afternoon tea.' So I have afternoon tea at five past one, and very good it is too.

Liverpool Street station is a building site and has been for two years, but we're in on time.

There then occurs something which could have put Passepartout, me and the astrologer out of business in a big way. Our Central Line train from Liverpool Street to Oxford Circus pulls into Tottenham Court Road station. No sooner have the doors slid open than a disembodied warning voice rings round the platform, which I notice with a shock is completely empty.

'Stay on the train! Stay on the train! There is a suspected package at the station. Stay on the train! Do *not* alight here.'

It's the first time that I've seen the Professor, a veteran traveller and hard man to scare, lose his colour. It drains from his face as I imagine it must be draining from mine. For a frozen moment we are stuck beside an empty platform far below the ground with a 'suspected package'.

We look at each other, the same thought crossing all our minds. After all we've been through. There is a moment's complete silence. Breaths are held. Then not a moment too soon, the doors swish closed.

After that London never recovers. It is like being back in the very pit of hell. At Oxford Circus the Christmas lights stretch away into the distance, and the Christmas spirit is similarly stretched. We attempt to film me buying a newspaper, to confirm my date of arrival, and are subjected to a volley of abuse from the vendor such as we've experienced nowhere else on the journey. When we do buy a paper, the front page is full of grim pictures of the Clapham Rail disaster, which had happened as we were docking at Felixstowe. (All of us were sobered by the thought that if we had taken the Le Havre–Southampton ferry we could quite possibly have been on one of those trains.)

We hurry through the crowds down Regent Street, and at five

minutes to five, shabby, tired, rushed and ruffled I stand before the steps of the Reform Club, seventy-nine days and seven hours since I had walked down them to go round the world. Would love to have bought Passepartout a drink, but we weren't allowed inside.

A *See pages 123–124 for related activities.*

Activities

Beginnings

The three extracts in this section deal with the reasons for making journeys and the preparations for them. Wonder and curiosity are the greatest motives for travel. Katie Hickman expresses these forcibly and makes us all long to explore the forbidden, lost land of Bhutan. Adventurous challenges motivate Michael Palin and Tony Hawks: for Palin they are an excuse to show the world on television, allowing us to share the adventures; for Hawks, comedy takes on a serious purpose in troubled Ireland.

Close reading

Setting Off: Michael Palin

1   In what various ways does Palin contrast himself and his team with Phileas Fogg and Passepartout from Jules Verne's novel?
2   What are the impressive features of the Orient Express?
3   Find some everyday details of the initial train and ship journey that contrast with the splendour of the Orient Express.
4   Palin enlivens his description of the journey with dryly humorous details and comic quotations from other people he meets. Find examples of these.
5   Palin is a sharply observant descriptive writer. Study the sentences on the Reform Club (pages 10 to 11) and Boulogne (page 14). Which adjectives and verbs create the impressions?

A Forbidden Land: Katie Hickman

1   How exactly did Katie Hickman get the idea to visit Bhutan?
2   Why does she think that Charles Lamb missed the point about travel books? Why is she fascinated by travel?
3   What are the remarkable features of Bhutan? What do its various names suggest?
4   Why does Bhutan guard its independence so fiercely?
5   Why does Hickman want to go there?

All For a Bet: Tony Hawks
Hawks writes about a weird travel idea with charm and vitality. Instead of laughing at him, we identify with him and become involved in the strange challenge.

1   What impressions do Hawks and Shane have of each other?
2   Look at Hawks's first 'meeting' with his fridge. Which words and phrases create the humour here?
3   Why is Gerry Ryan interested in Hawks's story?

4   What benefits for Ireland does Gerry see in the 'purposeless' but 'fine' idea for a journey?

Writing

I   'We travel,' says Katie Hickman, 'to rediscover the mysteries that are in life.' Robert Louis Stevenson wrote a poem about such dream places:

> I should like to rise and go
> Where the golden apples grow;
> Where beneath another sky
> Parrot islands anchored lie …
> Where in sunlight reaching out
> Eastern cities, miles about,
> Are with mosque and minaret
> Among sandy gardens set …
> Where are forests, hot as fire,
> Wide as England, tall as a spire …
> Where among the desert sands
> Some deserted city stands …

Imagine some wonderful places that you would like to visit. Use Stevenson's first line to start and write a poem or prose sketches. Adjectives, colours and comparisons are the secrets of success here.

2    Imagine members of a family or friends are preparing for a journey, and are discussing where they would like to travel and what practical preparations they would make. In pairs or small groups write this as a dialogue or script, or tackle it as a spoken activity.

3   What did Katie Hickman experience in Bhutan? Imagine what she saw, heard and enjoyed during one day.

 Speaking and listening work

113

Sights and Sounds

Richard Burton, a writer who lived in Shakespeare's time, famously said that travel 'charms our senses with such unspeakable and sweet variety'. The person who never travels is 'a kind of prisoner ... that from his cradle to his old age beholds the same still; still, still the same, the same!' The traveller sees the world freshly. All his senses are vividly alive in a new environment. He is captivated by the exotic surface of the new place, the colour, the apparent difference of foreign life and customs. The passages in the 'Sights and Sounds' section deal with this magical aspect of travel.

Close reading

Paradise in the Panjshir Valley: Eric Newby

I   As Eric Newby sits at tea, what strange things does he see in the little town by the bridge?

2   The scene changes as he enters the Panjshir Gorge. Which of his senses does Newby use to create the atmosphere of the place?

3   He comes to a mountain valley that seems like 'paradise'. Which details of the life and people there support this idea?

4   Finally he comes to a town, Ruka. What features of the place impress him?

Port of Spain, Trinidad: V.S. Naipaul

V.S. Naipaul concentrates on the sounds of Port of Spain that express its overwhelming vitality.

I   'Yet it is forbidden to talk' is an example of humorous exaggeration: there is no actual rule against talking in Port of Spain. Find other examples of exaggeration in the long opening paragraph.

2   Naipaul drives up a hill to view the city. What details does he choose to show how it appears below him?

3   What sounds does he become aware of as he looks down?

Nyika Plateau: Sir Laurens van der Post

I   Sir Laurens van der Post emphasises the wonderful peace of the African bush. What comparisons help to establish this?

2   The huge landscape is made even more dramatic by the wild life. The arrival of the leopard is exciting. Which adjectives and adverbs, and what comparisons, create the picture of the animal?

3   The charge of the zebra is, again, described through comparisons. What are these and which is most effective?

4   Why does Michael not shoot the zebra?

In Samarkand: Natalia Makarova

I In this passage, the delights of travel spring from the wonderful historic architecture and brilliant street market of an ancient legendary city. How does Makarova use the following to convey the wonder of Samarkand?
  • colour
  • comparisons
  • details from history.

2 In what ways does the Samarkand market contrast with those of St Petersburg and Moscow?

Festival Time in Seville: Jan Morris

For Jan Morris, the people and the customs of a foreign society are the most wonderful aspect of travel. She delights in Seville's Feria which draws all age groups and classes into its astonishing colour and energy.

I Reread the third paragraph. Pick out the key words and phrases that build up to the climax of the 'explosion' of the Feria.

2 What are the various purposes of the Feria?

3 Look at the fifth paragraph. Which adjectives, adverbs, comparisons or descriptive phrases express the glamour of the people?

4 The evenings are full of sounds. What are these?

5 What are Morris's and the city's feelings when the Feria is over?

Writing

I Write an impressionistic description of a holiday place (preferably abroad) that you have visited. To add drama, write in the present tense ('It is early morning. I am going … '). Use detail observed through your five senses in imitation of the passages in 'Sights and Sounds'. You are already *in* the place so leave out travel details. Divide your piece into contrasting sections, for example morning in the town, afternoon on the beach, evening watching the night life of the streets. Do not forget to use vivid adjectives, adverbs and comparisons, as in the passages you have studied.

2 Travel writers are fond of lists to help put across rapid impressions of a place and its atmosphere (Eric Newby's descriptions on pages 28 and 29 are good examples). Divide your observations into short sentences or use semicolons as Newby does. Adjectives are a key to success here – remember to include colours.

3 Your piece might turn into a poem. Here is an extract from 'Summer Journey' (about a Spanish holiday) by W.R. Rodgers:

> Sunday morning, seven by the clock,
> And the village silent except for the cock
> Ricocheting far away: and over the roof

Are the dark Pyrenees, overweening and aloof
As ever. A boy comes into the square
And a pigeon rises and flashes the rosy air.
Never was morning so clear. And one by one
A rope of bees bubbles up into the sun.
A bell is calling the people to early mass ...

Write a miniature poem about a place. Choose three or four remembered details from what you have seen, heard and, perhaps, touched in that place. Try to put across its essence or its atmosphere. To give you some ideas, here is an example by the late Victorian poet, Arthur Symons, writing about the French seaside resort of Dieppe:

At Dieppe
After sunset

The sea lies quieted beneath
    The after-sunset flush
That leaves upon the heaped grey clouds
    The grape's faint purple blush.

Pale, from a little space in heaven
    Of delicate ivory,
The sickle-moon and one gold star
    Look down upon the sea.

Speaking and listening

I   🗩 Discuss, in a group, the five passages in 'Sights and Sounds'. What are the strengths and weaknesses of each extract? Which is the most effective as travel writing?

🗩 Speaking and listening work

Buses, Bikes and Trains

Writing in the 1820s, the poet Samuel Taylor Coleridge made fun of the British craze for tourism after the Napoleonic Wars had finished and Europe was once more open to the traveller. All kinds of transport were taking people abroad: it was the dawning of the age of popular travel.

> *Keep moving! Steam, or gas, or stage,*
> *Hold, cabin, steerage, hencoop's cage –*
> *For move you must! 'Tis now the rage ...*

Trains, bicycles, buses, cars and aircraft have developed this restlessness a thousandfold. The writers of the passages in 'Buses, Bikes and Trains' attach their observation of foreign lands to these easy – and not so easy – methods of travel which have opened up the world to all of us.

Basket Search in Burma: Rory MacLean

1   It would have been easy to fly to Mandalay. What does Rory MacLean see as the disadvantages of flying to a travel destination? Why choose to go by bus?

2   The bus journey shocks MacLean. What are its discomforts?

3   'Dichotomy' means a division into two, or two ways of seeing one subject. What is the dichotomy that MacLean sees in the Burmese people?

4   Use details from the passage to create a little prose or poem sketch about what can be seen of Burma from the bus. Start: 'We begin at dawn ... ' Do not forget to include the colours, the discomforts, the food and the sign!

Seeking Miss Small: Irma Kurtz

A Greyhound bus offers more comfort than the Burmese Isuzu but it leads to places, like Elwood, Indiana, that seem just as bleak as grimly-ruled Burma.

1   What was the point of Irma Kurtz's visit to Indianapolis? What are the charms of the city and its surroundings?

2   She has preconceptions of Elwood, where her mother grew up. How does the reality of the town contrast with these?

3   What does the conversation in the cemetery add to the impression of the town's life?

4   What were the darker sides of life in Elwood when Kurtz's mother was young? Why is she so intent on answering her mother's old teacher?

An Unusual Proposal: Stanley Stewart

Travel makes you aware of the laws, written and unwritten, and customs and bureaucracy of other societies. Stewart discovers this when he tries to buy a train ticket in China.

1   What is 'guanxi' and how does it work?

2   Buying a railway ticket is like going to church – how exactly?

3 How does Stewart fight against 'meiyou', the 'no' given to him at the ticket office?

4 How does he finally purchase his ticket?

The Highest Railway in the World: Paul Theroux
Paul Theroux chooses to explore South America using some of the most fantastic railway lines in the world. On the high mountain line to Huancayo, he almost literally runs out of air to breathe.

1 What are the ugly features of life in Lima, Peru?

2 What beautiful things does Theroux observe as the train climbs the mountain?

3 All this beauty is ruined by altitude sickness. What are the worst effects of this on the travellers?

4 How does Theroux contrast the glory of the line's engineering with the people and settlements on its route?

5 Theroux's night in Huancayo is one of the dark times familiar to all travellers. Why is John Donne's sermon not particularly appropriate reading at such a time?

Bicycle Buying in Hungary: Dervla Murphy
The purchase of a bicycle in Hungary allows the author to show the clumsy complexity of a life still coloured by the old-style communist state.

1 What are the surprising complications of buying a bicycle in the Szivarvany store?

2 Why are Budapest's streets so dangerous?

3 What are the dismal features of no. 17–21 Egressy ut.?

4 How did Dervla Murphy finally get her bicycle assembled?

5 Murphy finally sets off on her Rumanian tour. What are the difficulties of cycling in Rumania? Which of these is most impressively described to us?

Chinese Bicycle Torture: Anon
This prize-winning anecdote concisely sums up the problems of hiring a bike in China.

1 Why is bike-hire such a problem?

2 What are the dangers of Chinese traffic?

3 How do language problems contribute to the conclusion of the story?

Writing

1 Write about a journey you have undertaken, perhaps on holiday or on a school visit. Make clear the excitements and the problems you experienced with your methods of transport.

2 Most travellers enjoy watching the world from the windows of coach, car,

train or plane. Write your impressions of things seen on a journey. Robert Louis Stevenson's poem 'From a Railway Carriage' might give you some ideas:

All of the sights of the hill and the plain
Fly as thick as driving rain;
Here is a child who clambers and scrambles,
All by himself and gathering brambles;
Here is a tramp who stands and gazes;
And there is the green for stringing the daisies! ...
And here is a mill, and there is a river:
Each a glimpse and gone for ever ...

Speaking and listening

1 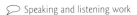 Discuss the strengths and weaknesses of various methods of transport used in travel. Which allows you to come closest to the foreign country?

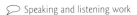 Speaking and listening work

Water!

A senior United Nations official, visiting London on a very wet day, was asked what he thought of the weather. 'A country that has rain is very fortunate,' he replied. He had seen the world and knew, as do travel writers, how precious water is for human activity and for life itself. The four passages in 'Water!' deal with the pleasure of water in a tourists' playground, and, more grimly, with the threat of too little water and the danger of too much.

Underwater, Down Under: Bill Bryson
Bryson writes as an American tourist in Australia, exploring one of the most splendid natural wonders of the world, the Great Barrier Reef. His droll, sceptical notes on the tourist's way of life are silenced by the wonder of the underwater spectacle.

1 Why is Bryson at first reluctant to visit the Reef?
2 How does the coach driver add to his fears?
3 'Hard not to be impressed,' admits Bryson. Why are the statistics about the Reef remarkable?
4 The submersible voyage finally wins Bryson over. He describes it with deft skill. Find examples of the following, which all contribute to the vivid picture:
   • adjectives   • comparisons
   • adverbs   • exotic names
   • verbs.
5 Ocean swimming proves too much for Bryson. What problems and dangers does he encounter?

Mrs Puri's Plumbing: William Dalrymple
Water is almost always in short supply in India, except during the torrential downpours of the September monsoon. William Dalrymple shows us life in a water-scarce society, revealing the courage, humour and eccentricity of Indian people that he encounters in it.

1 What impression of the September monsoon is given on pages 79 and 82?
2 What does Darymple tell us about his peculiar flat?
3 How does water play a part in his life there?
4 Mrs Puri and her husband are strongly portrayed characters whom Dalrymple admires. Write character sketches of them using details from the text.
5 What do we learn about the history and society of India from the life stories of Mr and Mrs Puri?
6 What are the servants like and what do they do? What is the point of having these servants?

The Takla Makan Desert: Sven Hedin
This diary is typical of many accounts of hardship endured by nineteenth-century travellers and explorers. Sven Hedin sought out the most difficult places as a challenge to himself. Here he shows a desperate struggle to survive in a near waterless world.

1   What does Hedin tell us about the wonder of the desert night?
2   What desperate measures do the men take to escape thirst?
3   The journey is a 'funeral procession' as the travellers die, one by one. How do Hedin and Kasim try to escape the heat among the desert sands?
4   What grim joke is told by the footprints in the sand?
5   How does Hedin make his final discovery of water so dramatic?

The Aswan Dam: Stanley Stewart
At Wadi Halfa in Sudan, Stewart sees a great irony: a desert community suffering from too much water as the old town is drowned by the new Aswan Dam lake.

1   What picture of new Wadi Halfa and its life is given on pages 89–90?
2   What is the routine of life at the hotel? What are its attractive features?
3   What memories are there of the charms of old Wadi Halfa?
4   Which details create the drama of the flooding of the old town?

Writing

1   Write about pleasures connected with water – the sea, lakes or rivers – as you have experienced them on holidays. Reread 'Underwater, Down Under' for inspiration. Sensory details, colours and sounds will make your description more exciting.
2   Compare 'Mrs Puri's Plumbing' and 'The Aswan Dam' as pictures of life in developing countries. How do the charm and energy of the people contrast with their difficult surroundings?
3   Read over the last part of 'The Takla Makan Desert'. Compare this with the poem below which is by another nineteenth-century traveller, the poet Wilfred Scawen Blunt. How does each piece create the drama of discovering water? Which is more forceful?

> The Oasis Of Sidi Khaled
>
> How the earth burns! Each pebble underfoot
> Is as a living thing with power to wound.
> The white sand quivers, and the footfall mute
> Of the slow camels strikes but gives no sound,
> As though they walked on flame, not solid ground.
> 'Tis noon, and the beasts' shadows even have fled

Back to their feet, and there is fire around
And fire beneath, and overhead the sun.
Pitiful heaven! What is this we view?
Tall trees, a river, pools, where swallows fly,
Thickets of oleander where doves coo,
Shades, deep as midnight, greenness for tired eyes.
Hark, how the light winds in the palm-tops sigh.
Oh this is rest. Oh this is paradise.

Homecomings

The three passages in 'Homecomings' deal with the complicated ideas and feelings connected with coming home from long journeys. After the restlessness and endless variety of travel, there is the longing for stability and familiarity. Whatever the beauties of the foreign cities and landscapes, ordinary, closely known places have a special magic. Returning also offers a chance to look back on travel, to reflect on its excitements and its difficulties.

Close reading
Finis: Peter Fleming

1 For Peter Fleming the 'supreme moment' of homecoming is undermined by the commonplace talk of the other passengers. Can you identify types of people from what they say? What kind of things do they talk about? How does Fleming want them to behave on such an occasion?

2 The irritations of other people lead Fleming to discuss with himself the advantages and disadvantages of travelling alone:
   • What is his point about hair and honey?
   • Why is it easier to adapt to a foreign way of life alone?
   • What effect do disagreements have on travellers' enjoyment of foreign places?
   • What is Fleming's conclusion about travel?

Kathmandu and Home to Delhi: Vikram Seth
Vikram Seth chooses the long way home from his Chinese university to his home in Delhi in India. He finally tires of the wonders of China, Tibet and Nepal and flies the last section of the journey. This passage describes the wonder and the fatigue of travel. Seth writes in the present tense so that we can share his observations and reflections more immediately.

1 How does Seth use the following in creating his picture of Kathmandu?
   • strange and colourful people and happenings
   • contrasts
   • sounds
   • tastes.
   Find examples of each.

2 Why does Seth feel growing impatience with his long journey?

3 Why are the fluteseller and the sound of the flute so important to him?

4 His reflections on flute music allow him to see benefits of his long journey. What are these?

5 Quzha, Sui and Norbu are Chinese people that Seth has met on his journey. How do such meetings help to improve international relations?

6 Seth finally sees that air travel, although quick and convenient, has disadvantages. What are they?

Full Circle: Michael Palin

In Jules Verne's novel, Phileas Fogg races around the world in 80 days to win a bet, starting and finishing at the Reform Club in London. Michael Palin, Fogg's imitator, also races against the clock on the last part of his long, round-the-world journey. Fogg burned the wooden fittings of his Atlantic steamer to win his bet with a second to spare; Palin has seventeen hours to spare but there is plenty of drama before he reaches the steps of the Reform Club. Palin has the qualities of a good travel writer: curiosity, sensitivity to atmosphere and sharp observation of detail.

1 What are the attractive, and unattractive, features of Le Havre?
2 How do the travellers show their good humour and comradeship in the last part of the voyage?
3 What are Palin's first impressions of England? Which key adjective does he repeat?
4 As he leaves the ship, he feels sympathy for sailors. What does he admire about them and their work?
5 What does he think of London?
6 What are the final dramatic twists of the journey?

Writing

1 Write about a return journey home after a holiday. Describe the departure for home, the journey and the arrival at your house. Include the contrast of the holiday place and your familiar home. Bring in your feelings about travel and the return. Write about the people involved in the journey.
2 Many poets have written about the traveller's longing for home. To James Elroy Flecker, writing in the early twentieth century, the splendours of Switzerland suddenly meant nothing:

> Mine be the ancient song of Travellers:
> I hate this glittering land where nothing stirs:
> I would go back, for I would see again
> Mountains less vast, a less abundant plain,
> The Northern Cliffs clean-swept with driven foam,
> And the rose-garden of my gracious home.

Write a poem or a short piece of prose about a traveller's thoughts of home. What exactly would he or she miss? Try to be precise about sensory details.

Speaking and listening

1 ▷ Hold a debate with speakers for and against the following sentiment: East, West, Home's best!

▷ Speaking and listening work

Acknowledgements

The publishers gratefully acknowledge the following for permission to reproduce copyright material. Every effort has been made to trace copyright holders, but in some cases has proved impossible. The publishers would be happy to hear from any copyright holder that has not been acknowledged.

Around the World in 80 Days by Michael Palin. Reproduced with permission of BBC Worldwide Limited. © Copyright Michael Palin 1989

Dreams of the Peaceful Dragon by Katie Hickman, published by Victor Gollancz. Reprinted with permission of Orion Publishing Group Limited

Round Ireland with a Fridge by Tony Hawks, published by Ebury Press. Reprinted with permission of The Random House Group Limited

A Short Walk in the Hindu Kush by Eric Newby, published by Secker & Warburg. Used by permission of The Random House Group Limited

The Middle Passage by V.S. Naipaul (Penguin Books 1969) © Copyright V.S. Naipaul 1962. Reprinted with permission of Penguin Books Limited

'From St Petersburg to Tashkent' by Natalia Makarova, from *Great Railway Journeys of the World* reproduced with permission of BBC Worldwide Limited. © Copyright Natalia Makarova 1994

Spain by Jan Morris, published by Faber and Faber Limited. Reprinted with permission of A.P. Watt Limited

Ventures to the Interior by Laurens van de Post, published by Chatto & Windus. Reprinted with permission of The Random House Group Limited

Under the Dragon by Rory MacLean, published by HarperCollins*Publishers*. Reprinted with permission of the publishers

The Great American Bus Ride by Irma Kurtz, published by Simon & Schuster Inc. Copyright Irma Kurtz 1993. Reprinted by kind permission of the author and The Lisa Eveleigh Agency

The Frontiers of Heaven by Stanley Stewart, published by John Murray (Publishers) Limited. Reprinted with permission of the publishers